"Jay and Laura Laffoon ignite sparks of inspiration on and off the platform. They are extraordinary communicators who are hilariously funny, gut-level honest, and right on target with practical wisdom that helps all of us to make marriage a celebration every day. This book should be required reading for every married couple!"

—**Carol Kent**, speaker and author,
A New Kind of Normal

"I've stood at the back of a room packed full of couples, laughing, nodding and writing notes as they watched an incredibly talented couple help them light (or reignite) that 'spark' in their marriage. That couple was Jay and Laura Laffoon, and what they shared with several hundred couples that day is now captured in this book—ready to spark great things in your relationship. If you're ready to gain some serious warmth and light in your home, read this book. It will spark as much closeness and caring for you as it did for my wife, Cindy, and me."

—**John Trent**, president, The Center for StrongFamilies;
author, *The Blessing* and *The 2 Degree Difference*

"For years, Jay and Laura Laffoon have been helping couples ignite the Spark at their Celebrate Your Marriage conferences. Now they've done it in a book. Read this and watch the sparks fly!"

—**Kevin Leman**, author, *Sheet Music*

"Jay and Laura have hit a homerun. Not only does this book give practical, biblical advice, it does it with the usual charm, grace, and humor that Jay and Laura bring to their retreats. I highly recommend this book."

—**Jeff Allen**, comedian and author

"Jay and Laura Laffoon have written a candid and entertaining book on embracing and understanding intimacy in order to enjoy a successful and happy marriage. Life today is hectic and hurried, making it easy to disconnect from those you love. Oftentimes the first relationship to suffer is the one between a husband and wife. The Laffoons' book reminds us how important the five (yes, there are five!) facets of intimacy are in nurturing and strengthening the marriage bond. We laughed out loud as we identified with many of Jay and Laura's personal stories about their own marriage. The questions for reflection and discussion they include at the end of each chapter are much needed. Enjoy getting to know your spouse and your marriage all over again as you answer the questions. Your marriage can't help but benefit from the Laffoons' insightful, witty, and upbeat perspective on celebrating togetherness."

—**Eric and Jennifer Garcia**, Association of Marriage and Family Ministries

"Jay and Laura are a real couple living in the real world and now writing about real issues. For way too long Christians have been silent and let Satan run haywire with sex, and I celebrate a couple who will stand for God's principles of happy and holy sex! Way to go, Jay and Laura!"

—**Dan Seaborn**, president and founder, Winning At Home

THE SPARK

THE SPARK

Igniting the Passion, Mystery, and
Romance in *Your* Marriage

Jay and Laura Laffoon

BakerBooks
Grand Rapids, Michigan

Published by Baker Books
a division of Baker Publishing Group
P.O. Box 6287, Grand Rapids, MI 49516-6287
www.bakerbooks.com

Second printing, August 2008

Printed in the United States of America

Library of Congress Cataloging-in-Publication Data
Laffoon, Jay, 1961–
    The spark : igniting the passion, mystery, and romance in your marriage / Jay and Laura Laffoon.
      p.   cm.
    Includes bibliographical references.
    ISBN 978-0-8010-6831-7 (pbk.)
    1. Marriage—Religious aspects—Christianity. I. Laffoon, Laura, 1962– II. Title.
BV835.L25 2007
248.8′44—dc22
                                         2007041445

Authors are represented by the literary agency of The Nashville Agency, PO Box 110909, Nashville, TN 37222.

Contents

7

Acknowledgments

We want to thank the following people:

First, our children, Torrey and Grace. You two make life fun each and every day. Thanks for understanding when Mom and Dad are gone. God smiles when he thinks of you both.

Our families, who have supported us in everything we do over more than twenty years of marriage.

The board, staff, and volunteers of Celebrate Ministries, Inc. Your love and passion for ministry sustain us often.

The thousands of couples who have attended a Celebrate Your Marriage conference or workshop. You inspire us with your desire to work on this thing called marriage.

Our friends, our church family, and particularly our small group. Our nights of prayer, conflict, compassion, and "therapy" mean the world to us. It is not often that people find lifelong friends; it humbles us that we have so many.

Nashville Speakers Bureau, Tim Grable, Jonathan Clements, and Danny DeArmas. Thanks for believing in, supporting, and challenging us to be our best.

The wonderful folks at Baker Books, especially Chad Allen, for helping us make this project so much better than we could have by ourselves.

To Jesus—he's the only reason we're here!

Foreword

I sat in the back of the Grand Hotel Ballroom on Mackinac Island, Michigan, and watched with fascination as four hundred couples laughed and danced and sang the words to some goofy old hit tunes. This wasn't a room full of giddy teens. These were married couples of all ages, and they had come from all over the United States to celebrate their marriage. It was a party.

In the midst of all this hilarity a particular couple caught my eye. They appeared to have little to celebrate. They were not participating and turned slightly away from one another, not touching or smiling or making eye contact. In fact the sullen look on their faces advertised to anyone near that they were trying hard not to have fun. I remembered hearing them exchange harsh words during check-in. Evidently some conflict was inhibiting their ability to celebrate.

On the stage Jay and Laura Laffoon were doing what they do best—living out the give-and-take of marriage and having fun doing it. The spark of love burns bright in their lives.

Then Jay and Laura did or said something that brought the house down. I don't remember what it was. It really doesn't matter. What does matter is that the woman in this couple I mentioned started to smile. Oh, she tried to hide it with her hand, but she forgot to cover her eyes. (Eyes can smile too, you know.) Then she playfully punched her husband in the shoulder and before long they were engaged not only in the festivities but with each other too.

I have known Jay and Laura for years. "Passionate" is the best word I can think of to describe them. They argue and minister and parent and love with intense passion. And they use the flame of their passion for Christ and life and one another to ignite the spark of love in other marriages.

A can of butane sits in my garage. On the side it says, "Flammable! Keep away from any source of ignition!" When I abide by that rule, the can just sits there. It is useless. But when I put the butane in the right receptacle and intentionally expose it to a spark, it warms my house, lights a fine cigar, or floods my patio with light. It suddenly has purpose and impacts lives with joy and brilliance.

Too many marriages are just sitting on the shelf. No fire. No passion. No fun. The potential is there. All that's needed is a spark. This book you are about to read is the spark! Brace yourself for laughter and hope and love.

Ken Davis
President, Ken Davis Productions
www.kendavis.com

PART ONE

THE
SPARK

1

Our Story

How It All Began

The book of love has music in it
In fact that's where music comes from.

Peter Gabriel

Three Rules of Dating

On July 3, 1984, I (Jay) moved from my hometown of Petoskey, Michigan, to Atlanta, Georgia, to begin a job I secured after graduating from college. Exactly one day later mutual friends set me up on a blind date with Laura Elizabeth Bass.

We arrived at Laura's house thirty minutes early. At this point I became keenly aware of the first rule of dating: don't show up a half hour early! I knocked on the door for what seemed like an eternity. After each knock, I turned to Chaz and Deaver (the couple who set up this date) and stared in disbelief. *Is this girl standing me up before we've even met?* My self-esteem was withering by the millisecond.

We were just about to leave when the door swung open. The next moment is a bit of a blur. I remember being surprised, and I remember seeing a young woman who had obviously just gotten out of the shower. Her hair was soaking wet and strung all over her face. She stood before us in nothing but a T-shirt and boxer shorts, clutching a towel to her chest in an obvious attempt at modesty.

I stuck out my hand and with every bit of personality I could muster said, "Hi, I'm Jay." Laura let out an embarrassed, junior-high giggle and promptly turned toward Deaver with a look that sent chills down my spine. Now that I think about it, since then that look has been aimed at me a time or two . . . or a thousand.

Chaz and I went into the living room and turned on TBS; I think we watched *The Andy Griffith Show*. Deaver went with Laura while she got ready. Twenty minutes later I learned the second rule of dating: when women go away together, miracles happen. I looked up and saw beauty. The shower-soaked woman I met at the door had been transformed. I was dumbfounded.

The four of us went to an Atlanta Braves game. I vividly remember that I paid too much for the tickets, that the food was awful, and that Laura and I talked about everything. I had spent time with many members of the opposite sex before. In fact, some of my best friends were women, but this was different. The conversation flowed like a mighty river. The current ran deep and strong. I was amazed by the intensity so early in the relationship.

When the game ended, the lights in the stadium went dark and the Fourth of July fireworks lit up the sky, eliciting

the usual oohs and aahs. After the finale, Chaz grabbed
Deaver's hand and bolted for the gate to beat the crowd.
Deaver instinctively grabbed Laura's hand, and in turn
Laura grabbed mine.

My heart leaped out of my chest. It was at that moment
that I first felt "the spark."

It was strange. I've held many girls' hands before, but
this made my entire body feel like it was going into a
seizure. My arms, legs, and head felt like they were reel-
ing in every direction because of the ecstasy. It scared
me to death.

I quietly analyzed the situation the entire trip home.
That may be why Laura got out of the car so quickly. Not
so much as a goodnight handshake. I learned later that the
next morning when Laura's mom asked her how the date
went, Laura replied without hesitation, "Mom, I'm going
to marry that man!"

Over the next ten days I learned the third and final rule of
dating: if a woman wants to marry you, give up! They should
teach a course for men in every college across America
called "Give Up 101." It would save us all a tremendous
amount of pain and suffering.

In a city of two million people, Laura managed to have
our paths cross eight of the next ten days. I didn't know it
at the time, but we have a word for this now—it's called
stalking! To this day I don't know how she did it.

The coup d'état took place when she invited me on
a weekend trip to the mountains with her friends. That
Saturday night, ten days after our blind date, in a log
cabin on a mountain in North Carolina, I asked Laura
Elizabeth Bass to be my wife. Her reply: "What took you
so long?"

The Ring

Three hundred dollars! That was all the money I had in the world. I moved to Atlanta, paid my first month's rent, and had three hundred bucks left over. I had told Laura I couldn't afford a ring yet, and she assured me it was okay.

I appreciated her graciousness, but I wanted to give her a ring. To me a ring was a symbol of my love and commitment to her. I couldn't wait for the moment when I could slide that symbol onto her finger. That moment, it turned out, was not far off.

The day after I asked Laura to be my wife was a day from heaven: Carolina blue sky, billowing clouds, and my new fiancée sitting beside me as we drove back to Atlanta. I lay in bed that night with my heart on fire. I was in love, and nothing else in the world mattered. That is, until Monday morning.

As soon as I got to work, I knew something had changed. I had been there less than two weeks, but I could tell something big was going down. The company I had come to Atlanta to work for, the reason I moved a thousand miles away from home, was closing its doors. I was out of work.

My life turned upside down and inside out. I was in love, but I had no job, no money, and no place to live. As Dickens so aptly put it, "It was the best of times; it was the worst of times."

What would I tell Laura? What would I tell my parents?

Laura was gracious once again. "First," she said with a smile, "I have money; second, you can live with my mom if you need to; and the ring . . . well, I'll get it when I get it. Now kiss me!" WHAT A WOMAN! At that moment I knew why I had moved to Atlanta. It was to begin the rest of my life with the woman my mom had been praying for since I was a child. I truly felt peace in the midst of the storm.

I called home, and before I could relay the news Mom said, "I'm so glad you called. I've got some business to cover with you." She proceeded to tell me of a life insurance policy she and Dad had taken out for me years before. She told me I could keep it or cash it in. Hmmm, I thought . . . cash! I didn't know why we hadn't covered this bit of business before I left home, but the thought of $2,000 in my grubby little palms was just the news I needed.

Then it was time. "Mom," I said, "put Dad on the other phone. I've got some good news and some bad news." I told them about Laura, and—

"JAY WILLIAM LAFFOON, YOU DO NOT TELL YOUR MOTHER OVER THE PHONE THAT YOU'RE ENGAGED AFTER KNOWING THIS GIRL ONLY TEN DAYS! I certainly hope this is the bad news."

I winced. "Well, Mom, actually that was the good news." Silence. Dead air. Nothing.

"We trust you, son. Go on." Dad's voice was like a bell ringing on the steeple of a church, comforting and encouraging.

As we talked, I began to revel in the fact that the insurance issue was just now coming up. God's timing is perfect!

If I had wanted, I could have scraped by on $2,000 for quite some time, but I was a man on a mission. That money was my ticket to an engagement ring, and nothing would stand in my way.

After days of shopping, I purchased the ring and devised a plan to give it to Laura on top of a mountain in Quaker Ridge Camp near Woodland Park, Colorado. Every summer my dad brought kids from Michigan to this high adventure camp. Laura and I were going to join them for the week. Soldier's Mountain lies on the backside of the range that runs beside the U.S. Air Force Academy. The view from the top of Soldier's Mountain is nothing short of spectacular: a picture postcard of Pike's Peak and the surrounding mountain ranges. And at the peak is a cross made from pine trees wedged between two large rocks. I would give Laura the ring on top of Soldier's Mountain, at the foot of the cross.

To put it mildly, I was excited. Laura and I drove from Atlanta to Colorado Springs with very few stops. We slept an hour in a rest area in western Kansas until the sunrise woke us, and we were on our way again.

I had hidden the ring and a bottle of champagne, given to me by the diamond store, in Laura's backpack instead of mine, figuring it would be the last place she would look. My idea was to order two pan pizzas from a Pizza Hut in Woodland Park and hike to the top of Soldier's Mountain. After we had enjoyed our pizza and bubbly, I'd give her the ring.

The hike up Soldier's Mountain takes about twenty minutes, depending on your physical condition and the number of times you stop to take picture after picture of this place touched by the hand of God. I kept pushing to get to the top. "You've got to see it; you've just got to see it," I kept saying. Laura, on the other hand, reminded me we had just driven twenty-four hours straight, gotten little sleep, and were now operating at over 8,000 feet above sea level.

About halfway up, I saw something moving down the trail toward us at a rapid speed. We stepped to the side. Here in the middle of Pike's Peak National Forest, a bear or mountain lion was not at all out of the question, and neither would make for good company.

But the view cleared, and bounding down the trail came a twelve-year-old boy. He was running so fast he was nearly out of control. From fifty feet away he yelled, "Are you Jay Laffoon?" "Yes!" I hollered back, and by the time I answered he was twenty feet past me bellowing, "Goood!" not even breaking stride.

My best friend in the world was Dean Moyer, a college bud who moved to Atlanta to work for the same now-defunct company I had just left. He had phoned ahead and arranged for a single red rose and a card to be delivered to the foot of the cross on the top of the mountain. Laura got to the cross first and saw the rose. "Hey, there's a flower," she said with her sweet Southern drawl.

"Have a look," I said.

"Oh, it has a card."

"Interesting. What does it say?"

She read its message aloud: "Congratulations, Jay and Laura. Love, Dean." She looked confused. "What do you suppose that means?"

My plan was unraveling before my eyes, so I had to think quickly. "Oh, Dean's always doing things like this. He's just congratulating us on climbing the mountain. Awfully nice of him." I paused, waiting for a reply, hoping she bought my story. "Oh, isn't that sweet?" At that moment I was very, very thankful Laura had been a cheerleader in college. Whoosh—right over her head.

We had just gotten out of our car and climbed over a thousand feet to the top of this mountain and were at an altitude of 8,500 feet. There we had consumed the pizza, which was now cold, and the champagne, which was warm. We sat with our legs dangling over the edge of the cliff with the cross above us and looked out over the marvelous landscape that was being drenched by the noontime sun.

The moment had arrived.

I reached into the backpack and pulled out the jewelry box. Opening it and holding it out toward Laura, I said, "Honey, I know I've asked you this, and I know you said *yes*, but I want to make it official. Will you marry me?"

At that moment her bottom lip began to quiver. It was cute at first, but I now know what that quiver means. Sweat began to bead up on her forehead. I'd never seen Laura sweat before. I now know what that sweat means. The look on her face was puzzling, like it was caught halfway between extreme joy and agony. I now know what that look means.

Nothing came out of her mouth for what seemed like an eternity. Nervously I asked again, "Honey? Will you marry me?"

At that moment something came out of her mouth, but it was not the word *yes*. This woman I loved, this woman I was asking to marry me, this woman I wanted to spend the rest of my life with began to spew an uninterrupted stream of pizza, champagne, and gastrointestinal juices. Laura was puking her guts all over me!

Does this mean yes? I wondered.

She could have sent it over the edge of the cliff; she could have turned her head the other way; but no, she had to barf all over me. Immediately she began to laugh. At first I failed to find the humor, but slowly a smile crept over my face as she put the ring on her finger and hugged me, all covered with goop. "YES, YES, YES, YES, YES! Don't you know that in the South a woman must puke on a man before she can marry him?"

We wiped the remains off the corners of her mouth and off the front of me. I will never forget that day, or that smell.

"The spark" had ignited the passion, the romance, and the mystery of why Laura felt the need to puke.

Let the fire burn!

2

Why This Book?

Introducing Intimacy

Laura and I were married in 1984, and to make a long story short, in May of 1996 we hosted our first Celebrate Your Marriage conference. Working in youth ministry together for the first twenty years of our marriage, we never dreamed we would be considered marriage experts. But working with teens and their parents led us to see the importance of strong, healthy, fun marriages. Eventually we felt called to minister to married couples. Our hope today is for every married couple to learn to celebrate their marriage. To that end we offer tools to help married couples see and experience marriage as a lifelong journey of adventure and joy.

Over the past decade of marriage ministry we have noticed a

> *Our hope today is for every married couple to learn to celebrate their marriage.*

trend in what married people hope to receive from us. Men, wanting to better understand their spouses, come to us hoping we have Ph.D.s in "wifeology." Women secretly wish we could give their husbands a shot of "Casanova-cain" to recapture the magic they felt while dating. Married couples look to us with pleading eyes, hoping we can help them regain the wild affection they once felt for each other.

Because of our desire to help couples find true intimacy in their marriage, we conducted a survey of over two thousand married people, asking them to share their views on intimacy. In addition, we conducted an in-depth survey with nearly one hundred married people delving deeply into the issues of intimacy. We felt we needed to know the problems, issues, and challenges most commonly faced by couples before we could help them.

Throughout this book we will be addressing needs and issues brought forth from the survey. As you read through the quotes and comments, we hope you will be able to relate to many of the universal experiences. Take heart in the knowledge that we all share similar joys and challenges. As Jay's mom says, "In marriage you will struggle with three things: money, sex, and in-laws."

Intimacy is something we all long for because it is powerful and life-changing. It is also elusive. We don't know when it will show up or how long it will last. In fact, no one understands intimacy when they fall in love. We certainly didn't. We just heard the music in our hearts and started to dance.

> Jay's mom says, "In marriage you will struggle with three things: money, sex, and in-laws."

Intimacy is the spark. The spark starts small and grows with time into a burning flame of love. Over the years, how that fire is stoked will determine the depth of your relationship and the joy you experience together. To keep the fires of love alive, careful attention must be paid to all five facets of intimacy: social, mental, emotional, physical, and spiritual. Each of these facets is key to igniting the passion, romance, and mystery in your marriage.

Priorities

The young people at the FCA golf camp were excited to hear Joe Schumer, owner of and PGA teaching pro at The Pines golf course in Weidman, Michigan. They were filled with anticipation because Joe was going to demonstrate the proper way to hit a bunker shot. I (Jay), on the other hand, couldn't wait to hear Joe talk about his faith. He becomes giddy when talking about Jesus. He didn't disappoint.

Near the end of his demonstration, Joe mentioned something in passing that hit me like a slap on the face. Joe said, "Here are my priorities: (1) God, (2) my wife, (3) my children." In that moment it was as if all the neurons in my brain started firing at once, and I concluded that most Christians really have their priorities screwed up.

Ask typical Christians (male or female) to share their priorities and they will say: (1) God, (2) family. Do you see the slight but essential difference in what Joe said and what most of us would say? Mark 10:8 reads, "The two will become one flesh." It *does not* read, "The two will become one flesh until the kids come along, and then they become part of us too." Here is where we make our mistake: not realizing that our relationship with our spouse is completely distinct from our relationship with our children and the rest

> *Our relationship with our spouse is completely distinct from our relationship with our children and the rest of our family.*

of our family. While they may overlap, our first and primary relationship after God is with our spouse, and as a result our children must come later.

Our wrongly configured priorities materialize in many dysfunctional ways. An obvious example is parents who spend all their time chauffeuring, coaching, or watching children play insane amounts of sports or other activities. Instead of using our time in these ways, we should be building the intimacy God ordained as his first institution—marriage. Our children must come third. While this flies in the face of so much evangelical thought today, the single best thing you can do for your child outside of having an authentic walk with Christ is to make your marriage a priority.

Some of you might be saying, "But we enjoy watching our child play basketball, and as a result, it draws us closer as a couple." *Yeah right!* How can sitting in a crowded gym with no opportunity to really connect, surrounded by others who are passively observing sports, bring you closer as a couple?

> *The single best thing you can do for your child outside of having an authentic walk with Christ is to make your marriage a priority.*

Now don't get us wrong. Children need encouragement and support from Mom and Dad. We attend many of our kids' functions. But what your kids and ours *don't* need are parents who are out three or four nights a week at the expense of a deeper, healthier marriage relationship.

Unlocking Celebration

We wrote this book for anyone who wants to experience intimacy in their marriage. The main message is simple: we believe the key to unlocking celebration in your marriage begins with something we all desire—intimacy. Building and developing intimacy will help you celebrate your marriage.

Intimacy is a tough subject because it means so many things to different people. Often in our conferences we'll ask the ladies to shout words that define intimacy for them. *Closeness, hugging, talking,* and *cuddling* are frequent answers and all very good. Ask men the same question and you will hear them reply in unison: *sex!*

Ah, there's the rub—for each person, intimacy is spoken and lived out differently. For Laura intimacy is best realized in time alone with Jay. For Jay intimacy is what happens when Laura initiates physical contact of any kind: holding hands, a foot rub, kissing, or . . .

This book is designed to help you and your spouse go beyond physical and emotional intimacy to build intimacy in every area of marriage. Each facet is essential in developing authentic intimacy:

social intimacy
mental intimacy
emotional intimacy
physical intimacy
spiritual intimacy

Don't put too much pressure on yourself. Laugh with each other and realize no one gets it right all the time. Most likely

> *We believe the key to unlocking celebration in your marriage begins with something we all desire —intimacy.*

27

you are deeply intimate in one or more of the facets listed above. Rejoice; be glad! Then take a serious look at the areas that need improvement and begin working on the proven ways we offer to strengthen those areas.

Don't take yourself too seriously; just realize you're both human and won't always get it right. One time a man came to us and said he remembered his first marriage retreat with his wife because it was such a disaster. The leader of the retreat asked, "Can you name your wife's favorite flower?" He turned to her and asked, "Pillsbury, isn't it?" It went downhill from there.

When we were dating our spouse-to-be, we thought he or she was perfect. After the honeymoon we realized this perfect mate changed overnight and did not clear it with us first! Those habits that were cute when we were dating quickly became annoying. We can all look at our spouses and see what we wish we could change. In a successful marriage we accept those idiosyncrasies and don't spend too much energy on trying to change that which we cannot.

As a young teenager, I (Laura) spent many hours babysitting. I loved children and was passionate about babysitting. The mothers who employed me were firm about one thing: after you put the baby to bed, do not get her up again. If she cries, let her cry. After twenty minutes, if she was still crying, I could check that the baby was okay and pat her back. But I could not get her up out of bed.

This was the best training I could have received. When Jay and I had our first child, Torrey, I remembered this training. I put Torrey to bed and, of course, he cried. I waited twenty minutes, checked on him, made sure he wasn't hurt, hungry, or wet, rubbed his back, and then left. Inevitably he fell fast asleep. This process of allowing our baby to cry drove Jay crazy! He desperately wanted to go in and get

Torrey up out of bed, rock him, feed him, coddle him. I said *no* and was firm about it. We went round after round. Finally, after many nights of watching what I was doing and seeing that soon Torrey did not even cry when he

> *An important part of marriage is accepting the things we would rather change.*

was put to bed, Jay realized I had been trained well.

At first Jay wanted me to *change*, but as time passed he recognized the benefit of allowing me to be the mother God had trained me to be during those years of babysitting. Jay showed maturity in our relationship by accepting me rather than insisting I change.

When you are young and you watch a romantic movie, you really think that is what life will be like! You watch a TV husband and wife sleeping all cozy next to each other, appearing to be the perfect couple who never drool in their sleep, snore, or make other strange sounds. When the TV couple awakens, they open their eyes, smiling adoringly at each other, and kiss good morning. What a crock of hooey! What about morning breath, bedhead hair, and those lovely morning volcanic eruptions from that perfect man or woman next to you? An important part of marriage is accepting the things we would rather change.

In the first part of this book we will look at the purpose of marriage and how growing intimacy in every facet of marriage will help the two of you become one. Becoming one is what turns the spark into the burning flame of love. In the second part of the book, we will detail some of the steps necessary to keep the home fires burning.

3

No Longer Two

Is There Such a Thing as Holy Sex?

I hope by now you see what this book is all about. We're going to laugh and have fun, but most importantly, we want to help you in your efforts to have a great marriage.

With so many different couples reading this book, most likely some of you have a marriage that is going great right now. Reading this book is a celebration of a terrific marriage because you want to keep it going. We understand that for some of you, however, life has thrown some bumps in the road and you're thinking, *We need to reconnect and get ourselves back on track.* Others of you think married life is rotten right now. You need time to focus and really sort out what marriage is all about.

We believe this book can meet each one of you at your point of need. Why? Because we're going to point you back to the author of celebration: Jesus Christ. We're going to explore how he can impact your marriage, not just today and tomorrow but every day of your life.

You see, we don't just want you to have a good marriage. We don't just want you to have a great marriage. We want you to have a *holy* marriage. We want to show you a way of being married that is totally different from what you might expect.

Along with that, we understand that even the subtitle of this particular chapter is going to set some of you on edge. But part of marriage is this thing called *sex*. No matter where you are on your life journey, it's a part of the whole picture. And frankly, we don't want you to have *good* sex. We don't even want you to have *great* sex. We want you to have *holy sex*.

Now you know what we do for a living: we sit around dreaming up really strange ways to get people to think and act regarding their marriage. As we were putting this chapter together and trying to define what it means to have holy sex, we kept thinking of a takeoff of the old Batman and Robin television show: "Holy sex, Jayman!" Sorry, we digress.

For some of you reading this book, *holy* and *sex* are two words you've never thought about putting together. We're telling you, no two words deserve each other more. God wants us to have *holy sex*. It's going to impact every aspect of our life. Unfortunately, many of us were brought up like our friend Ken Davis, who shares that his parents always taught him, "Sex is dirty, naughty, and disgusting, so save it for marriage!"

> *We want to show you a way of being married that is totally different from what you might expect.*

The Purpose of Marriage

Relax, holy sex isn't all about sex. Holy sex is about being *one*.

We love to ask couples, "What is the purpose of marriage?" Some of you may already be coming up with all kinds of answers in your head: procreation, companionship, fun, to find a "sugar daddy" or a "mommy dearest." Or if you're really spiritual, you might be saying that the purpose of marriage is to become like Christ.

We believe the purpose of marriage is to be *one*. It's not the sex; it's not the fun; it's not the companionship; it's not the sugar daddy or the mommy dearest. It is much more than that: the purpose of marriage is to be *one*.

Some of you reading this book might not be followers of Jesus. If that is the case, we hope you are pursuing what it means to follow him. (For more about what this means, see appendix B: "A Note from the Authors.") But for those who are passionate followers of Jesus Christ, as Laura and I are, you know that if he tells us the purpose of marriage, then that should be the purpose. Case closed.

So what does he say? In Mark 10:6–8 Jesus says, "But at the beginning of creation God 'made them male and female.' 'For this reason a man will leave his father and mother and be united to his wife, and the two will become one flesh.'" Now understand something. Up to this point, Jesus is quoting the Old Testament; every Jewish person knew this passage of Scripture. But then Jesus stops quoting the Old Testament and gives the purpose of marriage: "*So, they are no longer two, but one*" (emphasis added).

The purpose of marriage, then, according to Jesus Christ himself, is *to be one*.

> *The purpose of marriage is to be **one**.*

The Difference between *Oneness* and *Being One*

When we use the phrase *being one*, most Western minds think *oneness*, but the two are very different. *Oneness* is the perception that comes from sharing daily duties together. *Being one* is a state of the heart, soul, and mind.

When we discussed the difference between *oneness* and *being one* with our good friend Terre Grable, who is a professional counselor, she told us about a counseling technique she uses with couples. Terre talks to many couples who have not mastered what she terms the "institutional aspects" of marriage: figuring out who is going to assume which roles within the union (who is going to pay the bills, mow the lawn, bathe the kids, etc.).

We took that idea and discovered that a great way to discern the difference between *oneness* and *being one* is to understand the difference between the *institutional* aspects of marriage and the *mysterious* aspects of marriage. As we look at couples practicing the institution, we find people who live in the same house, pay the same bills, raise the same kids, maybe even go to the same movie together. While practicing these institutional aspects of marriage may bring a feeling of *oneness*, it does not constitute *being one*.

This is why so many couples wonder, "Is this really all there is to marriage?" This thought is the breeding ground for affairs. Men and women begin looking for fulfillment elsewhere because they have not become one with their spouse.

While the institution of marriage is mostly practical— figuring out who will pay the

> **Being one** is a state of the heart, soul, and mind.

bills, do the grocery shopping, mow the lawn, and clean the house—the mystery of marriage is more of an art. The art is revealed as we discover the heart, soul, and mind of our spouse and, at the same time, reveal ours in order to probe the depths of emotion, character, and love, which is truly *being one*.

Let's take a look at Scripture. The entire fifth chapter of Ephesians is encapsulated in the first four words: "Be imitators of God." Seems simple enough. A few verses later Paul gives us some practical advice: "But among you there must not be even a hint of sexual immorality, or of any kind of impurity, or of greed, because these are improper for God's holy people. Nor should there be obscenity, foolish talk or coarse joking, which are out of place, but rather thanksgiving" (Eph. 5:3–4).

Paul goes on to give us an illustration that makes us think on a profound level:

> In this same way, husbands ought to love their wives as their own bodies. He who loves his wife loves himself. After all, no one ever hated his own body, but he feeds and cares for it, just as Christ does the church—for we are members of his body. "For this reason a man will leave his father and mother and be united to his wife, and the two will become one flesh." This is a profound mystery—but I am talking about Christ and the church. However, each one of you also must love his wife as he loves himself, and the wife must respect her husband.
>
> Ephesians 5:28–33

Even Paul, one of the greatest theologians ever, could not fully comprehend this mystery called marriage any more than we can practically comprehend the mystery of Christ's church being one with him. This side of eternity none of

> *. . . that they may be one as we are one.*

us will ever have a lock on the art of being one. But the Lord has given us an opportunity to fulfill his prayer for his people: "That all of them may be one, Father, just as you are in me and I am in you. May they also be in us so that the world may believe that you have sent me. I have given them the glory that you gave me, that they may be one as we are one" (John 17:21–22).

It is our conviction that becoming one will never happen in the church, nor will it ever happen in our families, until it *first* happens in our marriages. Marriage is the model for the church, not the church for marriage. Marriage is the simplest form of church. "For where two or three come together in my name, there am I with them" (Matt. 18:20). Therefore, we must understand God's plan for becoming one with our spouse before we can impact the world for Christ. When we strive to become one in our marriage, it will spill over into every other relationship and aspect of our lives. Here is a practical illustration from the world of sports.

There Is No *I* in Football

The year was 1986, and the hype surrounding the NCAA Division I football championship was so big that the Fiesta Bowl was moved from New Year's Day to prime time on the evening of January 2. The title was going to be decided between two very different teams. Behind Heisman Trophy–winning quarterback Vinnie Testeverde, the number one ranked University of Miami Hurricanes was a flashy, superstar-ridden, offensive juggernaut putting up an average of thirty-eight points a game. In comparison, the number two ranked Nittany Lions of Penn State were the boring, uniformed version of a blue-collar plodder, their white with navy trim uniforms as dull as their game plan. Miami was the clear favorite.

I could tell you the winner before the game even started. You see, this was college football—one of the last and truest forms of a team sport. Miami came out for warm-ups with the names of the players embroidered on the backs of their uniforms. This made it easy to identify which superstar was making what amazing play. Penn State came out in their drab white and navy, and it struck me that there were *no names* on the back of their jerseys. I turned to Laura and said, "Penn State is going to win this one because they are a team." Sure enough, when the game was over, Testeverde had thrown five interceptions and the Nittany Lions prevailed 14–10.

So what does this have to do with being one? Plenty. You see, when you put on the "uniform" in marriage you put on a uniform that has no name on the back—no superstar husbands or Heisman Trophy wives. Sure you have an identity, but it's the team's identity, not your own. You are one.

The Beginning of Being One

Let us lay it on the line. Most men like sex. I mean REALLY like sex. In our work with couples we are finding about 20 percent of men have a lower sex drive than their wife, but by and large, most men really like making love to their wives.

Men are simple creatures. I tell Laura that I am as simple as a straight line: "Frankly, Honey, if I'm not asking you for a sandwich then, yep, I'm in the mood."

This is difficult for women to comprehend and results in the "boorish pig" label women attach to men. For whatever reason, God made man to desire to chase after his wife.

It has always been this way! Remember the playground? When our Grace was in second grade, our after-school conversation went something like this:

"How was your day?"

"It was great," she would reply. "We read books, did math, and played on the playground."

"What did you play on the playground?"

"We teased the boys until they started chasing us. Then they chased us until we got caught."

From the earliest ages, women love to be chased and men love the challenge of pursuit.

The Bible gives us a great metaphor. Spiritually speaking, Jesus (the bridegroom) is always chasing his church (the bride). "Here I am! I stand at the door and knock. If anyone hears my voice and opens the door, I will come in and eat with him, and he with me" (Rev. 3:20). Unfortunately the church often takes a long time to come around to desiring that deep relationship with Jesus.

We understand this concept in the spiritual realm, and we need to see the correlation to men and sex. We don't understand the *mystery* of why Christ (bridegroom) is always chasing the church (bride). In the same way there is no explaining the *mystery* of why a husband has such a strong desire to chase his wife!

This does explain why, for a man, sex is the beginning of being one. Whether consciously or unconsciously, a man's thinking goes something like this: *wow, was that great! I can't believe this beautiful creature actually wants to have sex with me. She's incredible, and I want to get to know her even better so maybe we can do that again.*

True Confessions of a Happy, Happy Man!

Laura and I had sex last night. I don't tell you that in some voyeuristic, sicko way. I tell you that so you will understand what I've been doing today while writing this part of the book.

Laura is away today speaking for a MOPS (Mothers of Preschoolers) group. We have just gotten back from one weekend retreat and are heading to another this Friday. The laundry is piled high, dirty dishes are stacked in the sink, and there is no plan for dinner. As I kissed her good-bye at 6:30 a.m., I decided that I was going to do the laundry, wash the dishes, and fix dinner today. Why? Because I am a happy, happy man!

There is *nothing* I wouldn't do for my wife after we've had sex. I want to please her in every way possible. I want to get to know her better and pursue her so that, yes, we might do *that* again.

True Confessions of a Happy, Happy Woman!

While Jay's "happy, happy day" was the day after having sex, mine (Laura's) was the day leading up to it. You see, we had sex that night because it had been a good day. We had worked in the morning, together. We had a lunch date. We laughed, talked, and had a great day! For a woman, sex is the culmination of *being one*. Here is an often-heard cliché that I think definitely applies: "For a man, when all is right in the bedroom, all is right in the world. For a woman, when all is right in the world, all is right in the bedroom." Do you see how that works? For a man, being one begins in the bedroom and then the rest of his world is right. For a woman it is just the opposite. Being one begins outside the bedroom.

Being one for a woman is a process. I liken it to kitchen appliances. Women are Crock-Pots; they are slow cookers. You have to plug them in first thing in the morning, and they take all day to cook. Men, on the other hand, are like microwaves—punch the right buttons and they are ready to go!

We will discuss this further in chapter 7 when we talk about physical intimacy and its impact on being one. As we look at being one, we cannot overlook the primary way we express being one.

The impact of holy sex on marriage

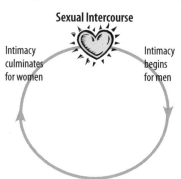

The Impact of Holy Sex on Marriage

So how does holy sex—being one—impact marriage? In every way. As a couple discovers the depth and satisfaction that come from being one, life and daily routines take on new and exciting meaning. He no longer mows the lawn out of obligation, and she no longer cleans the house out of duty. We do these things in order to discover more of the mystery as we travel the road of shaping our marriage into what God intends. No longer is it Jay and Laura, who happen to be married, but the marriage of Jay and Laura, a single entity designed in heaven and lived out for the glory of God. So how do we achieve holy sex? How do we achieve being one?

We like to think of it as the *intimacy dance*. Dancing is one of the most intimate actions on the planet. That's why we don't want our teenagers doing it! Picture the scene: face-to-face, moving together, not saying a word, and yet knowing exactly what the other is thinking and feeling. That's intimacy.

One thing we have found is that the only way you can dance is if you are living in the moment. You don't dance in the past; you don't dance in the future; you dance right now.

A couple can dance as two separate individuals stepping on each other's toes, not sure who is leading, looking uncomfortable and awkward. Or a couple can dance as two individuals who have come together intentionally, moving together as one, each doing their part of the dance seamlessly, meshed together, music in motion.

Fire dances too! We have all sat around a campfire entranced by the dancing flames. A beautiful ballet choreographed to perfection. Separate those flames by breaking up the logs and the flame soon dies. The same is true with the spark of intimacy. The five facets of intimacy are like the logs of a fire. As we intertwine our lives the flame grows and the fire burns brighter.

Time to set your marriage ablaze!

Questions for Reflection and Discussion

1. How would you describe the difference between oneness and being one?

2. On a scale of 1 to 10, rate the success you have of being one in your marriage.
3. What would you say is the purpose of marriage?
4. In the previous chapter, Jay shared the story of Joe Schumer, discussing the difference between a priority list of God first and family second versus God first, marriage second, kids third. Which priority list best describes you and why?
5. When do you feel most intimate with your spouse?

4

Social Intimacy

Strike the Match

I (Laura) suspect many of us have never thought about being socially intimate with our spouses. In fact, in our survey we frequently received this answer: "I'm not sure what you mean by 'social intimacy.'"

We begin dating and we enjoy this person's companionship. We have common interests. We are friends. Then somewhere along the line we fall in love. For some it happens quickly; for others it happens over time, but we begin to discover that we've become more than friends. We become lovers. For some reason when this happens, very often we cease being friends.

Here are some answers to our survey question, "What keeps you from dating your spouse?"

"Time mostly—not making our date time a priority."

"Making the time. We have it, just don't make it."

"I usually spend my time alone, usually associated with work."

"Honestly, we use time (too many things going on) as our primary excuse/obstacle. But really the biggest obstacle is in not making it a top priority. I don't think about it often to take the initiative to plan a date. She is way better at this than I."

We stand at the altar and say "I do." The marriage begins. Life settles in, careers, cars to buy, a mortgage, and obligations. Children are born, more obligations. Careers take off, and responsibilities rise. Suddenly we discover that our friendship as well as the time to nurture it no longer exists. Oh sure, we have friends—just not each other!

Here are some quotes from our survey of people who do not feel their spouse is their friend anymore:

"Often I don't feel 'socially intimate' because when he is with his friends, he is WITH his friends. We have talked, discussed, even argued over this matter. I sometimes feel 'abandoned' by him even though we may be in the same room. He is trying to work on this, ONLY if I mention it."

"We have not been married very long, but I think that it has gone down (friendship)."

"Lack of feeling like it's something we really want or need to do for 'us.' We've been having a lot of family issues that have tended to push us apart. The early closeness we had is very shaky a good part of the time. Glad to say that things are improving and we are working on our problems instead of being pulled away from them."

Love defined by the experts—children

Carrie, age 5: "Love is when a girl puts on perfume, and a boy puts on shaving cologne, and they go out and smell each other."

Crissy, age 6: "Love is when you go out to eat and give somebody most of your french fries without making them give you any of theirs."

Danny, age 7: "Love is when Mommy makes coffee for Daddy and she takes a sip before giving it to him to make sure it tastes okay."

Emily, age 8: "Love is when you kiss all the time, then when you get tired of kissing, you still want to be together and you talk more. Mommy and Daddy are like that. They look gross when they kiss."

Chris, age 7: "Love is when Mommy sees Daddy smelly and sweaty and she still says he looks handsomer than Robert Redford."

Defining Social Intimacy

What exactly does social intimacy mean? Following are some thoughts from people to whom we posed that question:

"I love to feel her touch and for her to feel mine in public. Nothing nasty, just the arm around the waist or, uh, she can pet my head, mmm, love that. I'm more of a touchy person. Expressing my love to my wife is not something I have to think about."

"I'm guessing at what 'socially intimate' means. . . . I have felt surges of warmth and affection when Dave praises me to his friends in my presence. That's cool!"

"I think people can see that we are in love with each other. My husband is very demonstrative."

45

"When we have those 'stolen' moments of sneaking off alone and just talking."

"When we go to Home Depot or Lowe's and envision our dream home and what doors and windows we want."

"Sometimes at dinner, just looking into her eyes."

"When we are all alone, laying on the beach watching the water."

We think of social intimacy as dancing through life with your best friend. It is the process of recapturing, rejuvenating, and enjoying a friendship with your spouse.

The Initial Spark

When it comes to overall intimacy, the social intimacy facet is a good place to start because most of us, quite frankly, married our best friend. At least that is who you thought you married! When we date and eventually marry, we are looking for someone we enjoy being with and doing things with. We usually date someone for an extended period of time because we have common interests. Of course there is the physical attraction, but hopefully at the beginning we are focused on the social aspects of the relationship. As Laura and I got to know each other socially, we found there were some clear differences as well as common interests.

Laura grew up in a home with a diabetic dad, and as a result, she was used to well-balanced meals without much variety. Food for Laura was simple and plain. I, on the other hand, grew up in a home where meals were an event that was taken seriously. And often they were an opportunity to try something new: Hungarian goulash, Spanish rice, Austrian steak soup. It didn't matter where it came from, just how it tasted!

> *Social intimacy begins by blending many of the interests of your two lives into one.*

Within the first month of knowing each other we realized this was going to be a struggle. "I don't like ethnic food," Laura said. No Mexican, no Asian, no Indian, not even Canadian bacon for crying out loud! Then one day we were driving through the backwoods of Georgia with no civilization to be found and we were starving. Finally we stumbled across a mom-and-pop Mexican restaurant. It took a lot of convincing, but finally Laura agreed to go in.

The chips and salsa were homemade, and the cuisine was some of the finest to be found. Halfway through the fajitas Laura said, "So this is Mexican?" You see, it wasn't that Laura didn't like ethnic food; it was that she had never even *tried* it! Now Laura has been introduced to many of the fine foods from around the world.

Social intimacy begins by blending many of the interests of your two lives into one, just as we had to blend Jay's international palette with Laura's cautious palette. Then you take the next step and marry this person with whom you have many interests. This person means more than your fishing buddies or the girls you go shopping with. This person knows you better than anyone else in the world.

We asked some people to share what social intimacy looks like when it is fleshed out:

"We can be in a crowd and still be just the two of us."
"We both have a few things we do with close friends, but ultimately we enjoy spending our spare time together talking."

"When we are out having coffee or dinner in a relaxed atmosphere. The talk is deeper, and we are totally tuned in to what the other is saying."

"When we are taking a walk and just talking. When we get time away from the normal routine."

"Spending more time listening to each other."

"Socially intimate? Why every day! It might be a shared wink across a crowded room or dancing alone in our kitchen or walking the dog in the darkness."

"We love to do the same activities. We like variety and trying different things depending on our mood at a particular time."

Some of you are thinking, *That's not us.* But social intimacy is a great place to start for you, too, because you can come together socially as friends without putting too much pressure on the other facets of your relationship. The problem we see in too many marriages is that people believe marriage is a two-way street. If your marriage is a two-way street, then what you have are two cars racing past each other: zoom, zoom. Can anyone relate? Our lives become so wrapped up in the day-to-day that we lose the social intimacy we once had.

Terry and Deb lived marriage like a two-way street—two cars going in opposite directions. They were brought together through a mutual acquaintance in college and enjoyed each other's company. They were friends. They married, and life happened! They had no children, and each had their own job and many different hobbies. One hobby they had in common was golf. They enjoyed golf together during the summer and lived separate lives the rest of the year. Outside of the game of golf, they had lost their social intimacy. The separation was too much to overcome, and their marriage ended.

> *Marriage is not a two-way street; it is a one-way street.*

The other way a two-way street can go wrong is when two cars are on a collision course: zoom, crash. We pass, we kibitz, conflict, and collide. So we never spend time together because we are constantly annoyed or upset.

Marriage is not a two-way street; it is a one-way street. Not her way, not his way, but our way, the way God has designed for us. For people who struggle with that, we have devoted an entire chapter in our book *Make Love Everyday** to help couples define what God has created as "our way." You and your spouse are wired differently from how we (Jay and Laura) are wired. You are wired differently from how your friends are wired. God has created a way that is unique to you. In *Make Love Everyday* we help you determine the mission and purpose that God has given you and your marriage to create your one-way street.

Growing Your Marriage Friendship: How to Be Socially Intimate

We have all heard the maxim, "The couple who prays together stays together." We would like to add, "The couple who *plays* together stays together." Social intimacy is the foundation to a great marriage: playing together, enjoying each other's company, taking a walk, test-driving a car.

A simple way to build social intimacy into your marriage is to spend time together. It seems obvious, but for some reason when we get married we can forget to date. It can be a struggle to find time to spend together and nurture social intimacy.

*Jay and Laura Laffoon, *Make Love Everyday* (Phoenix: ACW Press, 2002).

A Simple yet Practical Idea

Jay and I like to do dissimilar things, so when date night comes, we each want to do something different. To overcome this struggle, we each wrote down our five best dates (keeping within our budget, mind you). Then we meshed them to create a series of great dates.

Laura's five great dates:

- shopping
- going for a walk
- shopping
- joining a book group
- shopping

Jay's five great dates:

- dining out
- golfing
- dancing lessons
- golfing
- cooking lessons

We meshed shopping and dining out by combining dinner out with a shopping trip to the mall. When we go golfing, while Jay hits range balls and practices putting, I browse the pro shop looking for deals on shirts, shorts, and accessories. When we signed up for dancing lessons, we had to go shopping for tap shoes. And of course walking is a great form of exercise we can throw into our golf dates.

Now it is your turn. Take your five great dates individually and then mesh them together. They will become your great date arsenal.

Spend time together focusing on each other.

We are not asking you to be joined at the hip and totally disregard your personal interests, hobbies, and friends. What we are saying can be summed up best with this quote from our in-depth survey: "Movies, plays, dinner, walks . . . it doesn't matter; the important thing we do is spend time together focusing on each other and not the rest of the world."

The Principle of Staying One Ahead

One of my (Jay's) favorite characters that Johnny Carson used to perform was "Carnac the Magnificent." He could magically answer the question in the sealed envelope by simply holding the envelope to his forehead. The secret to Carnac's success was to always be one ahead. Johnny found out the answer to the first envelope before the show. After successfully answering the question before it was asked, he ripped open the envelope and revealed the question. For example, Carnac would hold an envelope to his head and say, "Barry Sanders." Then he'd rip it open and read, "Who is Jay's favorite football player of all time?"

Also on that sheet of paper was the answer to the next question. As he held the next envelope up to his head he simply remembered from the previous paper, "Chips and salsa," for example. Rrrrrrip. "What is Laura's favorite night-time snack?" You get the point.

We see this principle fleshed out each year at our conferences as roughly a third of the couples attending sign up for next year's conference before they leave the current one. They are planning social time into their marriage. Staying one ahead is a great way to keep your marriage tuned up. So as you finish one weekend or night or even afternoon away, begin planning your next so you can stay one ahead.

Attractors and Detractors

Each facet of intimacy is going to have attractors—those things that help that facet grow. Each facet will have detractors also—those things that hinder growth in that area. Children, work, time, money, friends, and priorities are just a few of the detractors to social intimacy.

> Harry and Donna attended every sporting event that their children participated in. This is a great way to support your children, but for Harry and Donna it was the *only* time they spent together. They were so consumed with their children's sports schedules that they never had time left for themselves as a couple.
>
> Barbara works full-time outside the home. She comes home every evening and does the daily chores of the household, prepares dinner, washes the dishes, and plans for the next day. Barbara spends her weekends catching up on the larger household tasks: laundry, cleaning, vacuuming. Barbara feels as if she never has time to go out with her husband.
>
> Lori and John are saving to buy a home. They pay all their bills at the end of the month, and all the rest goes into savings. They don't want to spend the extra cash to go on dates.

Detractors to social intimacy include:

- finances
- housework
- church responsibilities
- family needs
- workload

- time constraints
- child care
- lack of energy
- eBay and other websites
- kids' sports schedules
- health issues

Although there are many obstacles to social intimacy, there are also many benefits from taking the time to focus on this important aspect of marriage. Attractors to social intimacy include:

- date night
- couple friends and double dates
- shared activities
- developing mutual hobbies
- adventures
- day trips
- doing even menial errands together
- vacations, getaways
- meals out

Ralph and Julie have been married for forty-one years and are still best friends. If you asked if it has always been this way, they would tell you *no*. It has taken hard work and effort. As time has gone by and they have grown as individuals and as a couple, they have realized the importance of doing things together as well as with others.

I (Laura) remember when I first met Julie back in 1987. Jay and I had just moved to Michigan and were attending a local church in our community. The women of the church were going on a retreat for the weekend. Julie had become a friend of mine and attended the same church. I asked if she was going and she replied, "I have never been away from Ralph overnight."

I laughed. In twenty years of marriage they had not spent even one night apart! Right then I knew I needed to make sure Julie got a life. She was going on that trip.

Julie went on the retreat that weekend, and she had a blast; Ralph survived as well. Over the twenty years since that retreat, Ralph now frequently enjoys golfing weekends with Jay and the boys. Julie and Laura—you guessed it—they shop! Our friends now have an understanding of the balance between individual social pursuits and building social intimacy as a couple.

Questions for Reflection and Discussion

1. From your perspective, rate the level of social intimacy in your marriage on a scale of 1 to 10.
2. What first attracted you to your spouse?
3. What common interests do you share?
4. How often do you date?
5. What detractors to social intimacy can you identify in your marriage?
6. What attractors to social intimacy can you identify in your marriage?
7. What would be your five great dates meshed together?
8. What is one way you can improve your social intimacy over the next twenty-one days?

5

Mental Intimacy

The Embers Glow

W e all can identify with the fact that we think differently from our spouse! For example, when Jay says, "Let's go into the city," he means, "Let's go test-drive cars." I (Laura) think he means, "Let's go shopping at the mall." When I say, "Let's take a nap," I mean, "Let's sleep." Jay thinks I am saying, "Hubba, hubba, hubba!"

Others who have recognized their differences put it this way:

> "I am much more intellectually driven. I enjoy learning. He considers himself to be inferior to me in that area."

> "I have more 'book smarts'; he has more 'street smarts.' . . . We don't connect much."

> "My husband and I both have graduate degrees, but since he has been retired and is working two fun, but

not intellectually stimulating, jobs, we seem to have a widening intellectual gap."

"As we grow closer, we understand each other so much more."

"He has become more aware of my needs, partly because there are less distractions, and of course he has been educated by me—HA!"

"Since the CYM conferences, we listen to each other more and respect each other's views. We didn't used to agree on things at all (i.e., raising children, politics, church). Now we listen and respect each other's views."

We Are Different on Purpose

It really didn't take me (Jay) long to figure out that Laura's brain operated very differently from mine. I remember moving into our first apartment and watching in amazement as she took her socks from a moving box and put them into her sock drawer. Her method of organization was similar to the way a tornado "organizes" a trailer park. She simply opened the box and threw them into the drawer. I was appalled and knew right away I needed to "fix" her.

You see, God has a plan for socks. We serve a God of order. Even Noah collected animals two by two: a simple lesson for the sock drawer! Or so I thought.

"That would simply take too much time," Laura responded in a tone that took me back to the snooty girls who picked on me in junior high.

"So how do you find the right socks?" I inquired.

"Let me demonstrate," she replied. Laura proceeded to push and shove her socks into the drawer. The number of socks she was trying to put in the drawer exceeded the fire marshal's maximum capacity by at least 50 percent. At this point she stood back, flexed at the knees, and flung the drawer open. Socks flew into the air in a rainbow of cotton. She grabbed two and shoved the rest back into the drawer. "See?"

> *When we began to accept our mental differences, we started experiencing the joy of mental intimacy.*

"Yes, I see that you have two socks that don't match!" I toyed.

Without hesitation she retorted, "They match close enough for ME!"

Over the years I have tried in a variety of ways to show Laura how a sock drawer should look: neat, organized, and color coordinated. But to no avail. Once I even bought her one of those sock drawer organizers with the little boxes where you put one pair in each box. The device is in her drawer to this day, drowning in a sea of unmatched socks.

Finally I realized that the way Laura kept her sock drawer was simply a function of the way her mind works. My mind is linear: step one, step two, step three. Laura's is random: steps, what steps? Neither way is right or wrong, just different, and when we began to accept our mental differences, we started experiencing the joy of mental intimacy.

Others who have understood the differences in each other talk about it this way:

> "We have come to respect our differences of opinion and enjoy the 'intense fellowship' when we don't."

> "We both excel and find interest in different areas, which is nice because then we can inform the other about what we've learned."

"We complement each other in intellectual areas very well. He is a Bible scholar, and I'm an educator."

"I think we push each other to think outside the box."

"Although I am a college graduate and my husband took technical training, I would definitely say he is smarter than I am. I would say overall we're pretty much equal."

A Couple Who Gets It

The mental intimacy facet is not always thinking the same thing at the same time. It is not always agreeing on items of discussion. It is not even who is smarter than whom. Rather, mental intimacy is your minds coming together in a connection that goes beyond intelligence or agreement.

Take Larry and Beth for example, a married couple we met at one of our conferences. Larry is a high school graduate. Beth has a master's degree in business. Larry went into the service straight out of high school. Coming out of the service, he had received training in computers that allowed him to pursue high-level computer jobs in the civilian world. Beth's master's degree has allowed her to follow her dream of owning her own business. Larry and Beth's differences in education have nothing to do with how intimate they are mentally. They read different styles of books, yet they share often about what they are reading and what they are learning. Larry and Beth both enjoy the computer yet use it for different pursuits. When a problem arises and needs to be solved, the two process the solution differently.

Larry and Beth are mentally intimate because they connect as people who are always trying to grow and learn in their own areas of interest. As they continue individually to grow and learn as people, they understand that the other is growing and learning as an individual, and they intentionally try to learn from each other.

Brain Scans

We spared no expense for this book. We had our brains scanned so that you can see what's going on inside our heads. Here's Laura's brain:

Laura's Brain

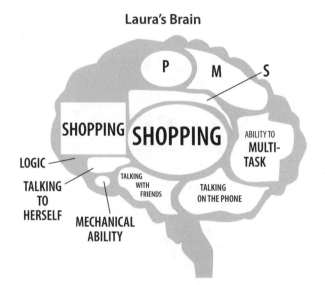

It's not hard to see that a large portion of Laura's brain is consumed with shopping. But then as we move to the back, you can see she's really good at multitasking: she can do many things at once. Then along the bottom, we have a theme going: talking on the phone, talking with friends, and then talking to herself. Someday she's going to be that lady at the grocery store walking through the aisles babbling to herself . . . oh wait, she already does that!

Laura does have some mechanical ability, but then you'll notice the logic "particle" in the front. Now across the top you see three random areas: the *P* area, the *M* area, and the *S* area. Normally these areas peacefully float around the brain, but every once in a while, oh, say about every thirty days or so, the three of them lock in together, and the Laffoon household finds itself hiding the sharp implements!

So let's take a look at Jay's brain scan:

Jay's Brain

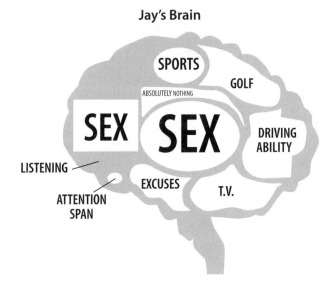

Umm . . . no explanation needed!

But seriously, if we're honest with ourselves and with each other, at some point in marriage you have either thought, "I'm really a lot dumber than my spouse," or, "I'm really a lot smarter than my spouse." Some may have had both thoughts at different times.

Howard Gardner, the John H. and Elisabeth A. Hobbs professor of Cognition and Education at the Harvard School of Education, is the author of over twenty books and is best known in education circles for his theory of multiple intelligences. He views intelligence as "the ability to solve problems, or to fashion products, that are valued in one or more cultural settings."* We have learned it doesn't matter

> *The issue is not how smart we are; it's* ***how*** *we are smart.*

who is smarter or dumber, because mental intimacy is not about smarts. You and your spouse both have brains; you're both intelligent. In other words, the issue is not how smart we are; it's *how* we are smart.

Defining Mental Intimacy

The following was written by a woman answering our survey.

> Eric didn't get the best grades in high school when we started dating. I never gave him the credit he deserved, assuming that he didn't measure up. Over the years, I have come to respect his thoughts so much more than I could have imagined. My father is someone I have always gone to for advice. He seems to be wise in all areas of life. And I almost always followed his advice. When we were dating and first married, I would find myself arguing with my husband, siding with my father's advice. We both generally tend to still value my dad's advice; however, I want Eric's insights first and foremost. And now there are even many times I don't go to Dad for a second opinion. Eric is very intellectually talented. It's just not math and music like me. It's politics, automotive, marketing, and business! I've come to respect him.

*Howard Gardner, *Frames of Mind: The Theory of Multiple Intelligences* (New York: Basic Books, 1983), x.

> *Mental intimacy is discovering, identifying, and appreciating the intelligence of your spouse.*

Mental intimacy is discovering, identifying, and appreciating the intelligence of your spouse. The woman in the story above had to realize that her husband is intelligent—maybe not in the ways her father is, but in his own way. When she discovered his intelligence and identified the areas of politics, automotive, marketing, and business, she then was able to defer to him and respect him.

Multiple Intelligences

Our job is to discover how our spouse is smart and then to defer to our spouse in that area—to be willing to say, "You know what, Honey? You are more intelligent in this area than I, so I will set aside my pride and allow you to really take the lead in this particular area." Howard Gardner identifies eight different types of intelligence,* and we'd like to share them with you so you can consider how they apply to yourself and your spouse. By determining who has more intelligence in these different areas, we can learn to defer to each other and increase the mental intimacy in our marriage.

Linguistic intelligence involves sensitivity to spoken and written language, the ability to learn languages, and the capacity to use language to accomplish certain goals. This intelligence includes the ability to effectively use language to express oneself rhetorically or poetically as well as a means to remember information. Writers, poets, lawyers,

*The information on the eight intelligences that follow is taken from Gardner, *Frames of Mind*.

and speakers are among those Gardner sees as having high linguistic intelligence.

More than likely, one of you is better with words than the other. You speak a little better, you read a little better, and you write a little better. You have linguistic intelligence.

We often run into our friends Gene and Carol Kent when we fly through Minneapolis. Since all four of us travel a lot on Northwest Airlines, it seems to be where we see each other the most! Carol is a phenomenal communicator who is in high demand as a conference speaker. Carol's linguistic intelligence is so strong that she is able to make a living through speaking.

Logical-mathematical intelligence consists of the capacity to analyze problems logically, carry out mathematical operations, and investigate issues scientifically. In Howard Gardner's words, it entails the ability to detect patterns, reason deductively, and think logically. This intelligence is most often associated with scientific and mathematical thinking.

This is the area where Laura needs some help. When I met her, she had had a checking account for two months and had already bounced fourteen checks. She thought, "It's a bank; they have money, don't they?"

Here's where the whole pride thing comes in. She grew up in a family that believed the woman is always supposed to pay the bills, but we know that in our relationship, when it comes to numbers, I'm the guy. If she hadn't laid down her pride, that mental intimacy would not have begun to grow and our relationship would have suffered on many levels. Because she is willing to defer to me in this area, we have a more financially secure future.

Spatial intelligence involves the potential to recognize and use the patterns of wide space and more confined areas. This is picture smarts. You're great with colors, dimension, and all the things that go into creating a picture.

This is where Laura is brilliant! She has beautifully decorated our home. The colors go together, the furniture coordinates, and everything is placed just wonderfully because she has an eye for space. Now if I were to be full of pride and demand, "No, I'm the man of the house, this is my castle," everything would be beige. How BORING! Because I was willing to lay aside my pride, our home is delightfully decorated and we have built tremendous trust mentally when it comes to decisions along these lines.

Bodily-kinesthetic intelligence entails the potential of using one's whole body or parts of the body to solve problems. It is the talent for using mental abilities to coordinate bodily movements. Howard Gardner sees mental and physical activity as related. Athletes have body intelligence.

As a chaplain for the PGA, on a weekly basis I (Jay) see firsthand people who possess this type of intelligence. Anyone who thinks that golf is a sport for nonathletes needs to join me on the course just once. A typical day for these men is to rise at 6:30 a.m. and head out to the practice green where they'll stroke a few putts. Then they're off to the range to warm up their full swing. After about an hour of stretching and warming up, they head out on the course for eighteen holes of golf. After a lunch break, they go out to the range to work on a particular part of their game and then spend another hour or more on the putting green. Finally, late in the afternoon they continue to their hotel or the nearest gym to work out for an hour or so. They make their living with their bodies!

Musical intelligence involves skill in the performance, composition, and appreciation of musical patterns. It encompasses the capacity to recognize and compose musical pitches, tones, and rhythms. According to Howard Gardner, musical intelligence runs in an almost structural parallel to linguistic intelligence.

Our son, Torrey, has a high degree of this type of intelligence. He plays guitar and has been blessed with his dad's musical ear and his mom's manual dexterity. As a result, he can hear a song once or twice and be able to play it. Many nights we'll be watching TV when a commercial comes on with some great music. We challenge Torrey to play that song, and before our show comes back on—voilà!

Interpersonal intelligence is concerned with the capacity to understand the intentions, motivations, and desires of other people. It allows us to work effectively with others. Educators, salespeople, religious and political leaders, and counselors all need a well-developed interpersonal intelligence. It is the ability to read people well.

Danny deArmas is a good friend and was one of the first people to really believe in the Celebrate Your Marriage ministry. Early on Danny did some management work for us, and one of his greatest gifts was reading people. Danny's dad was Cuban; he had fled to the States from Castro's regime. Danny's mom was a U.S. citizen. In their home Danny spoke Spanish to his father and English to his mother. He told us this made for some very interesting dinner conversations! Danny says his upbringing is the main reason he can read people so well. We will never forget one night Danny took us to Bongo's restaurant in Orlando, an authentic Cuban restaurant owned by musician Gloria Estefan. Our group of thirteen was told we would have about a forty-five-minute wait. Most of the group gathered in an area of the lobby, and three minutes later Danny came to report that our table was ready. He had stayed behind at the hostess station and somehow convinced the hostess to seat us promptly. Later

I asked him how much money he had to slip the hostess. He was almost insulted and explained that he simply communicated (in Spanish, of course) how important it was for us to get seated soon. I still don't know how he did it, but we had the best seats in the house!

Intrapersonal intelligence entails the capacity to understand oneself, to appreciate one's feelings, fears, and motivations. In Howard Gardner's view it involves having an effective working model of ourselves and being able to use such information to regulate our lives. People with intrapersonal intelligence are introspective and thoughtful.

Our daughter, Grace, is blessed with this form of intelligence; even at five years of age she felt and thought on a deep level. One night at the supper table she was complaining about everything from how her day went at school to her clothes not fitting right to what we were having for dinner.

I was fed up and slammed my hand on the table, asking, "Grace, do you know there are only two types of people in this world?" I was about to sermonize on the fact that people are either creators or complainers. You can't be both, and if she kept complaining she would end up a bitter, old woman!

No sooner had I asked the question than Grace responded, "Yes, Daddy, smart women and dumb men!" I couldn't respond to her inappropriate answer because I was on the floor doubled over laughing. Grace's internal thought process is not only deep but quick. Now who taught her that answer? Laura! Wit like Gracie's is one way intrapersonal intelligence is fleshed out.

One of Grace's favorite nighttime activities is to listen to an *Adventures in Odyssey* CD as she goes to sleep. One particular night before we put in the CD, Grace and I were discussing one of her friends who is a very smart and creative young lady. She and Grace are two peas in a pod! Grace was struggling with the fact that at times she feels inferior to her friend.

The next morning after Grace got dressed and was having her devotions she informed me that she was no longer struggling with comparing herself to her friend. She shared with me that the *Adventures in Odyssey* story the night before was about two friends who were always comparing themselves to each other, and the lesson was that God had created each of us unique, with our own gifts and abilities. Grace said she had learned that she did not have to compare herself to her friend because God had given each of them unique gifts and abilities. She left the house a much happier and confident little girl.

Finally, *naturalist intelligence* enables human beings to recognize, categorize, and draw upon certain features of the environment. It "combines a description of the core ability with a characterization of the role that many cultures value."* Folks with this kind of smarts love to be outdoors and in touch with nature.

I grew up in northern lower Michigan, which is an outdoorsman's paradise. Virtually every season of the year holds some type of fantastic outdoor activity, and the month of May brings out the morel mushrooms. These delicacies are found in the woods of northern Michigan in late spring and are almost as valuable as gold.

Willie Shoman, a friend of my parents, is a Native American and arguably the finest morel hunter on the planet. I will never forget the time Willie took my family to hunt morels.

Willie stood in one place and had us fan out in every direction. "Jim, there are five mushrooms ten feet to your

---

*Gardner, *Frames of Mind*.

right. Doyce, go over by that stump and look down to the left; you'll see four there. Diane, there's a couple by that fallen birch tree. Jay, take two steps forward and you'll see about eight of them."

"Where, Willie?"

"Right at your feet!"

"Where?"

"Stop! You're about to step on them!" He could see mushrooms from fifty feet away that I couldn't see when I was standing on top of them!

Choosing to Learn: How to Be Mentally Intimate

One of our survey respondents wrote the following insightful comment. We have italicized the parts we want to emphasize:

> I would honestly say that my spouse is more intelligent than I am, but over the years I have *discovered* that although he is a genius, there are areas that he has no clue about (although he can *learn if he chooses* to do so!), such as teaching a classroom of first graders! We have become *better listeners* and have *become more acquainted* with what each other is interested in, and from there this area has grown. When you care about someone, you *choose to learn* about what interests them and then you *learn* about that topic so you can have intelligent conversations about it or at least understand what the other is sharing with you as you listen.

Great advice. We cannot expect to become mentally intimate with our spouse without work. As this woman did, we have to *discover* our spouse's intelligence, *choose to learn*, *listen*, and *become acquainted* with his or her interests. We love that word *choose*. We have to make a deliberate choice to learn about our spouse, his or her interests, what makes our spouse tick, and how he or she is wired. Here are some others who realize how to be mentally intimate (again we have added italics for emphasis):

> *We have to make a deliberate choice to learn about our spouse, his or her interests, what makes our spouse tick, and how he or she is wired.*

"It took my husband time to *realize* how isolated he was in his 'ivory tower' environment. I also had to *realize* how our professions made him more isolated. I was *exposed* to things that were completely foreign to him and he had no chance of understanding without *explanation*."

"When we're traveling we often *read* marriage or parenting books aloud together and *discuss* them."

"She and I *share* almost identical values. I find it very easy to talk with her about most things. I help her understand politics; she helps me *understand* people."

Attractors and Detractors

In this area of mental intimacy, I (Laura) think the biggest detractor is the misconception that you must have the same level of education in order to be mentally on the same page. Education is not the issue. The issue is our attitude about intelligence and our willingness to defer to another individual who may understand a concept better than we do. Our attitude can be either a detractor or an attractor. If an individual has an attitude of superiority it will be a detractor, but if one understands multiple intelligences and has an attitude of deference, this can be an attractor.

Different learning styles can also be a detractor or attractor to mental intimacy. Jay and I learn differently. Jay learns by doing. I learn by reading and then doing. When we were putting together a stand for our golf bags, I read the instructions through one time and explained the steps we were going to take to achieve putting this stand together. He began putting the stand together, and I continued to read and explain as we went along. We got the stand built by working together in our different styles and letting each other work and make mistakes.

We build mental intimacy by realizing that as individuals we think differently, we process information differently, and we learn differently, and yet we must operate as one.

Questions for Reflection and Discussion

1. From your perspective, rate the level of mental intimacy in your marriage on a scale of 1 to 10.
2. Identify the way(s) in which you and your spouse are intelligent (using Howard Gardner's eight multiple intelligences).
3. Identify the areas in which you defer to your spouse's intelligence.
4. What detractors to mental intimacy can you identify in your marriage?
5. What attractors to mental intimacy can you identify in your marriage?
6. In what new way can you defer to your spouse's intelligence over the next twenty-one days?

6

Emotional Intimacy

Fanning the Flame

Over the years I have had the privilege of teaching a number of sales seminars for businesses. Clear communication is essential in sales. One basic fundamental of sales is this: "People buy on *emotion* and justify with the *facts*."

Think about your retirement for an example. Why do you sock money away for retirement? *Fear* of being without income. *Hope* of an income in your golden years. Not wanting to be a *burden* to your children. All good answers and all emotionally based.

The same is true in marriage. We "buy" into marriage because of the emotions we feel for our spouse. Then we justify (or sometimes don't jus- tify) staying with that person because of the facts. Maturing

> *People buy on* ***emotion*** *and justify with the* ***facts***.

and nurturing emotional intimacy in our marriage creates a constant "buy" into the union. The "facts" of our marriage become inconsequential when we realize how emotionally connected we continue to become.

What Is Emotional Intimacy?

Often when we think of emotion, we think of our souls—the seat of our emotions. We cannot be one without sharing our souls, and quite frankly this is what scares most of us men more than anything else.

The idea of sharing his emotions with his wife can bring shivers to any man's spine. But that is not necessarily emotional intimacy any more than sharing football scores will make your spouse a football fan. Emotional intimacy occurs when you understand and accept your spouse's emotional state. Notice we didn't say you had to *like* his or her emotional state, just understand and accept it.

Questions for Jesus

I (Laura) speak to women and couples all over the country, and I continually hear this, "I just wish he were more emotional." My response is, "He *is* emotional—just not like you!" God gave each of us emotions. As men and women we express these emotions differently, but even there we cannot assume stereotypes. In our marriage we often joke about Jay being more of a "girl" than I am. He wears his emotions right out on his shirtsleeve, and I tend to hold mine in check. At least I did until I turned forty.

I have a list of questions for Jesus when I get to heaven. The top one on my list is this: "What happens to a woman when she turns forty?" You see, when I turned forty I got achier and crankier. And I think I got crankier because

I got achier. I had issues.
For instance, I had eye-
lashes falling out and at-
taching themselves to my
chin. That will make you
cranky.

> *What happens to a woman when she turns forty?*

It used to be that I was the laid-back one in this relationship; Jay was a little more intense. But that all changed
when I turned forty. I became this emotional fireball that
could explode at the drop of a hat. It didn't matter who
dropped the hat or when, and it was different each day.

Chili Anyone?

Emotionally I (Jay) am pretty good at playing the blame
game. When I'm upset, sad, or angry it is ALWAYS someone
else's fault! Obviously that's not true. Certainly people can
hurt or upset me, but my emotional response to the situation is completely my responsibility. My mother saw this
trait in me from an early age, and she made me memorize
the phrase, "My response is my responsibility." Let me give
you an example.

One of the biggest blessings of our job is our commute:
thirteen to sixteen seconds from our kitchen to our library,
depending on whether you are traveling up or down the
stairs! As a result Laura and I often share lunch together,
and our favorite lunches are almost always leftovers. We
love to cook, and some nights I'm thinking about lunch the
next day before dinner is even digested.

Once on a snowy winter day Laura said she was going
to reheat some chili we had made the night before. The
cold, gray winter day was made for chili, and my mouth
began to water because, as everyone knows, chili always
tastes better on the second day. Laura not only made the

chili, but she created a lovely place setting for us with color-coordinated napkins and placemats. She lit a candle and put out a plate of crackers and cheese.

One thing you need to understand about me before we go any further is that I can't handle food that's too hot. I'm not talking spicy; I'm talking Fahrenheit! I have a tender tongue.

Laura called me down for lunch. We said the blessing, and I brought a spoonful of the delicacy I'd been anticipating to my mouth. Now I'm not saying you could hear my tongue sizzle like a sirloin, but it sure felt that way. I instinctively dropped the spoon and shoved the bowl away with full force. The bowl traveled two feet across the kitchen countertop and onto the floor as I screamed at the top of my lungs, "WHAT ARE YOU TRYING TO DO, KILL ME?"

Laura sat slowly shaking her head sipping chili with a little smirk on her face. That smirk angered me even more, and I retorted, "ARE YOU JUST GOING TO SIT THERE?"

"What would you like me to do?" she calmly replied. Emotionally I was convinced she was after the life insurance. Mentally I began to see the silliness of my actions.

The chili was now covering the floor and half of the oven door. I quickly began to take stock of what had just happened and realized some cold, hard facts. Laura had taken the time to make lunch. Not only did she make lunch but she also created a lovely and romantic setting in which to eat. As I cleaned up the chili and made myself a cheese and cracker lunch (there was no more chili), it hit me like a Mack truck that my overreaction had not only made a mess, it had unplugged Laura's physical intimacy Crock-Pot for that day!

We are all created emotional beings. How we express emotions, however, varies widely. Following are responses from people whom we asked, "Do you share your emotions with your spouse?"

"I don't share much. I never have with anyone. I more often keep things inside."

"Share? If I try to keep my feelings to myself, he finds a way to get me to open up."

"I share my feelings quite often verbally. He has his emotions written on his face and tone."

"I find it's best to keep my feelings to myself. He is very sensitive and takes things the wrong way a lot of the time."

"I share the negative feelings more often, when something is bothering me. He tends to share positive feelings more freely, but he usually withholds the negative feelings until there is a blowup."

All I Ever Needed to Know I Learned from My Dorm Mother

I (Laura) heard a phrase in college that I just love: "If you were both the same, one of you wouldn't be necessary." You decide which one (*wink, wink*). Seriously, though, if you both had the same emotional makeup, the same mental makeup, and the same social makeup, one of you wouldn't be needed.

We can't be the same. Ladies, you don't want your husband to express emotions the same way you do. You married a man, so why complain when he acts like one? And men, her emotions are real—as real as the adrenaline rush you get when that big buck is in your scope or the fish just took the bait. In

> *If you were both the same, one of you wouldn't be necessary.*

75

order to build emotional intimacy in your marriage, you must allow your spouse to be the person God created him or her to be.

True Confessions

I (Jay) want to start by saying that the following is just my opinion. I have no data to back this up, no studies to cite, just my observations and reflections. I believe that men feel emotions more intensely than women. "WHAT?" you might be saying. Yep, that's right. I believe when men feel—and the truth is they don't feel all the time, but when they do—it is on a deep level. Let me share some examples: Have you ever seen the joy and exhilaration of a man whose team just won the Super Bowl? Have you ever seen the anger and rage on the face of a man who's lived life on the street? You might be saying, Jay, those are extremes, and yes they are, but every man identifies with those extreme emotions and their depths. It's why *Die Hard* movies are so popular.

Women attach feeling to everything. They "feel" all the time and as a result get their feelings hurt easier, enjoy the little things in life more, and generally don't understand how a man can't answer the question, "Honey, how would you feel about winter white paint for the bedroom?"

Please don't get me wrong. I am not saying one way is right and one is wrong. I simply think a key component to building emotional intimacy is to understand these differences.

> *I believe that men feel emotions more intensely than women.*

When asked for an example of emotional intimacy, here is what some folks wrote:

"When I'm upset, I call my behavior 'processing'; she calls it sulking. Eventually, the dark cloud goes away and I open up more and more to share with my wife how I have been feeling. The word I use to describe my

> *I am not saying one way is right and one is wrong.*

feeling at this time would be that 'I'm mad.' On the flip side, words I use to describe positive emotions would be feeling 'good,' 'having a great day,' or a wink her way and an 'I love you.'"

"When I have had a terrible day with our son, when it gets to me, he knows that all I need is some support, even when all I can do is cry. My husband and I really do connect, and it's these times when I know that God has given me my soul mate. It's not always like that but more times than most."

"I think with all marriages you change—I think that you have to through submitting yourself to the Lord. He changes you, and you ask him to teach you to be a better spouse. It may be trial and error, but if you are willing the Lord directs you. Big changes have occurred as we talk. I think the most important change is that we have learned to talk and to listen."

"Here is the kicker: I know that he tries really hard, but I just have to let Christ fill in where he lacks. I love him very much, but emotions are not his strong suit. I had a friend tell me once that you cannot depend on husbands for all of your emotional support because they are bound to fail miserably. That is why we have mothers and friends to turn to when we need a good cry. But I promised long ago that never again would any unkind word pass my lips about my husband to my friends and especially my mom. I believe in self-fulfilling prophecy: if you say it, it will happen or get worse. I made too many mistakes with that when we were young and first married. I love my husband too much to disparage him to others. If I get those feelings I go to my heavenly Father in earnest prayer and I am comforted. Emotionally we are very different, but I have learned to work with what we have."

"I share my feelings when I know that it is a safe time, like not during the commercial of his favorite TV show. I used to share everything with him, and I have since realized that I do not have to. He doesn't care, and it really isn't his job to care. The important thing is that he cares about me, and if there is something that is important to our marriage or our family, then those are the feelings I share with him. When someone made me feel bad at the grocery store or my mom and I get into an argument, those are the things I call my girlfriends about."

Understanding Emotional Filters

We discussed earlier that we are all emotional beings; we just express emotions differently from each other. I would even go so far as to say that it does not necessarily have to do with whether you are male or female. I think it has more to do with your personality. I have met a lot of women who do not wear their emotions for the world to see, and I have met some men who do. Each of us has a filter that our emotions go through. When we can see life through our spouse's filter, we will understand his or her emotional makeup more clearly.

Emotional Filter of Loss

John lost a dear friend, a grandparent, and a childhood friend all in one year. Obviously he was seeing life through an emotional filter of pain and loss. Jane, his wife, recognized this and allowed John to experience the pain and loss and understood when that pain and loss sometimes colored other situations in their life, like overreacting with the kids.

The summer before I (Laura) met Jay, my dad passed away. While it has been twenty-three years since then, I still get very worried when anything goes awry with Jay's health, even if it is just a cough! My emotional filter at these times is loss and the fear of losing my spouse as my mom did.

Emotional Filter of Guilt

Early in their marriage, Sally and her husband moved back to the state where she had grown up. She began to feel guilty because her former boyfriend, with whom she had been intimate, was on her mind a lot.

Guilt from the past can be for things done or not done. This emotional filter can destroy a relationship if the husband and wife are not open and honest about the situation. Guilt can hamper our emotional intimacy as well as other facets of intimacy. A woman feeling guilty for thinking of another man may not believe she is worthy of the love of her husband. A man feeling guilty for perusing an inappropriate magazine may not feel worthy of his wife's affection.

Sally related her breakthrough: "As I shared my guilty feelings with my husband, he assured me it was normal due to the past sexual relationship." Because of his forgiveness and acceptance, "I never thought about it again."

Emotional Filter of Anger

A gentleman answering our survey describes his emotional filter of anger and pain in this way: "My father, a preacher for more than twenty years, left my mom for another woman. No one seemed to understand me but my wife. It was as if she felt every pain I felt. I love her for that."

Empathy, feeling your spouse's emotions, is the beginning of emotional intimacy. It is not expressing emotions in the same way as your spouse but rather identifying the emotional filter that is occurring at a particular time and feeling the pain, anger, loss, or guilt with your spouse.

Rock Bottom

Misty has been married eight years. She told us:

Right now we aren't even close to being emotionally intimate. You see, to my husband "feelings" are like the *F* word. He grew up in a family that *never* shared their feelings and *always* kept emotions bottled up inside. Very stoic.

Every time I try to share my feelings he calls me a little girl or says I'm being a selfish B———! I try to tell him how I feel about things and he says, "I can't help how you feel."

I just wish he would admit that everyone has feelings, including him. It would at least be a start in the right direction. I've never felt so unloved.

Each person's filter is different and can change repeatedly with life's circumstances. Years ago Jay's mom had cancer and was given only six weeks to live. God intervened, and ten years later she's still kickin'. That circumstance created emotional fear and sadness in all of Jay's family. Now, any time Doyce has an abnormality or needs a special procedure, all that fear and sadness flood back on Jay, his sister, and particularly his dad.

Recently, Doyce needed one of those procedures. After the doctor's visit and a good report, Jay's dad offered to buy lunch. Out of the blue, no special occasion, it was simply an outlet for the emotion and anxiety

> *Each person's filter is different and can change repeatedly with life's circumstances.*

that had been building over that procedure. Is Jay's dad a Christian? Yes! Does he trust that God is in control? Most definitely. But that doesn't negate the emotions we have as humans. Discover the emotional filter your spouse is using in a particular situation and begin to see the level of emotional intimacy in your marriage rise.

Emotional Energy

Besides understanding and accepting each other's emotions, it is important for a couple to be emotionally available for each other. The following story might help us understand this a little better.

We have a friend named Bill who didn't get married until he was forty-two. He married a wonderful woman who had also never been married. They wanted to have children right away, so they had a son within the first year. Then they waited a year and she became pregnant again, only this time they had twins. Within three years Bill had gotten married and had a son and two daughters.

A couple years later Bill said, "Jay, when I was single, I thought that if I saved enough time for my family, that would meet their needs." He continued, "What I've realized is that it's not about time. We all have the same amount of time in the day. I've learned it's about how much emotional energy I have saved for my family when

> *I've learned it's about how much emotional energy I have saved for my family when I come home at the end of the day.*

I come home at the end of the day."

That is so true. It's hard to work in any line of business these days without exerting an incredible amount of emotional energy. When we come home, it seems we have very little left for the people who need our emotional energy the most. My friend Bill told me point-blank, "Jay, I have had to learn to keep a reserve of emotional energy so that when I come home, I'm not just physically present but I'm engaging them as well."

It is not easy to save our emotional energy for those who need it the most. We have given of ourselves at work, and our emotional energy is gone. We come home, turn on the TV or computer, and are done connecting on an emotional level. Our emotional storehouse is empty. The challenge for couples to stay emotionally intimate involves intentionally keeping a daily reserve of emotional energy stored for each other.

Here are quotes from others who have made discoveries about emotional intimacy in their marriage:

"As we grow closer in our relationship with Jesus, our emotional relationship benefits."

"After the Celebrate Your Marriage conference we had a really nice heart-to-heart talk over dinner. I had never felt as connected to him, nor have I since, as I did during that moment."

"We are both widowed. Sometimes memories come flooding back and she wants to share them with me.

It can feel like all her memories are from her previous marriage until I realize that I do the same thing on other occasions."

"When I feel spiritually worn out she understands and helps strengthen me."

"We can connect easily if we pay attention to each other. But we can get lazy and miss the signals that are there."

"I am learning to think before speaking and not say the first thing that enters my mind. I need to be gentler with my words . . . less defensive . . . so that my husband will *want* to hear me."

Attractors and Detractors

As I (Laura) read through our survey results, I noticed one common theme when it came to discussing what attracted spouses in the area of emotional intimacy. *Sharing, interest, support, listening, empathy*—all words that describe *communication.*

Communication is the key to emotional intimacy. One survey respondent described this communication as being emotionally "naked" with each other. How many of us find it easier to be physically naked with our spouse as opposed to emotionally naked? Emotional nakedness requires vulnerability. It involves opening ourselves up to another person—the person who has promised to love, honor, and cherish us until death do us part.

Just last night Jay and I were watching one of those police dramas on TV—not one that would normally grab your emotions. This episode dealt with homeless mothers and children. At the conclusion of the show, I looked at my very normal, masculine husband and saw tears streaming down his face. He laughed a little as he wiped his tears. His vulnerability to allow me to see that this show had touched something inside him was an attractor for me.

There was also a recurring theme in the survey concerning detractors to emotional intimacy. *Avoidance, unawareness, unavailability,* and *disrespect* all point to one word—*apathy.*

> "Sometimes I don't think my feelings matter."
>
> "Sometimes, in all fairness, he doesn't have a clue about my feelings or what to do with them when he does know."
>
> "I internalize my feelings—makes for less stress."
>
> "More often he seems to think that my feelings are vastly overrated or unmerited given the situation. At the very least he does not feel that he is responsible in any way, even though something he said has hurt me."

When a spouse shows a lack of interest, for whatever reason, this is a sign to the other of apathy, which is the absence of concern or interest. I (Laura) have often tried to figure out why a spouse who has committed to love, honor, and cherish the other would be unconcerned or disinterested in his or her lover's feelings.

Maybe we become comfortable with each other. It is like the man who said to me, "Why do I need to tell her I love her every day? I told her when I married her. She should remember that."

I know for Jay and me it has only been recently that this has been an issue in our marriage, and I attribute it to my emotions dictated by hormones. Jay had a relatively even-keeled wife until

> *Communication is the key to emotional intimacy.*

she hit forty! After that it wasn't that he was apathetic as much as that he did not know how to handle all the emotions he was witnessing at one time. If Jay had been apathetic toward me, he would have acted as if these emotional outbursts were my problem and shown total disregard for me. Instead, he has sought to identify and try to understand what is going on in my world when "out-of-body hormonal experiences" happen.

> *Why would a spouse who has committed to love, honor, and cherish the other be unconcerned or disinterested in his or her lover's feelings?*

Questions for Reflection and Discussion

1. From your perspective, rate the level of emotional intimacy in your marriage on a scale of 1 to 10.
2. Identify the ways in which you and your spouse express emotions.
3. Think of the last "chili incident" you had in your marriage. What emotional filter were you utilizing to process at that time? What emotional filter was your spouse utilizing?
4. What common filters do you and your spouse utilize when processing emotion?
5. What detractors to emotional intimacy can you identify in your marriage?
6. What attractors to emotional intimacy can you identify in your marriage?
7. What is one way you can accept your spouse's common filter in the next twenty-one days?

7

Physical Intimacy

Hunka Hunka Burnin' Love

The fourth facet of intimacy—you knew we were going to get there—is physical intimacy. We have a top ten list of scientifically verifiable reasons you should have sex, just in case you need them.

The Ultimate Top Ten List

Number 10—Sex is a beauty treatment. Tests show that when women make love, they produce estrogen, which makes hair shine and skin smooth.

Number 9—Gentle, relaxed lovemaking reduces chances of suffering dermatitis, skin rashes, and blemishes. The sweat produced cleanses the pores and makes the skin glow.

Number 8—Lovemaking can burn up calories piled on during that romantic dinner.

Number 7—Sex is one of the safest sports. It stretches and tones almost every muscle in the body. It's more enjoyable than twenty laps, and you don't need special sneakers.

Number 6—Sex cures mild depression. It releases endorphins into the bloodstream, which produces a sense of euphoria and well-being.

Number 5—The more sex you have, the more you will be offered. Sexually active bodies give off greater quantities of pheromones, and those subtle sex perfumes drive the opposite sex crazy.

Number 4—Sex is the safest tranquilizer in the world. It is ten times more effective than Valium.

Number 3—Kissing each day keeps the dentist away. Kissing encourages saliva to wash food from the teeth and lowers levels of acid that cause decay, preventing plaque buildup.

Number 2—Lovemaking can unblock a stuffy nose. Sex is a natural antihistamine. It combats asthma and hay fever.

And the number 1 reason you should have sex—Sex actually relieves headaches! A lovemaking session releases the tension that restricts the blood vessels in the brain.

Gentlemen, I (Jay) am doing you a favor here. Next time your wife says, "Not tonight, Honey, I have a headache," you can reply, "You're in luck—I've got the cure."

The Importance of Physical Intimacy

All joking aside, physical intimacy is an important issue in marriage. It's something we struggle with and something we enjoy. But in order to build physical intimacy back into your marriage, you have to communicate about the intimate issues in life.

Real answers from real people on why physical intimacy is important:

> "Uhhh . . . I like it; she's beautiful and fun to be with."
>
> "I like to be held. I like it when my husband touches me when he passes by. I like to 'soak up his atmosphere.'"
>
> "Sometimes I just want to be close to him and feel loved."
>
> "I love her like a fat kid loves cake. I've always been touchy. It's my love language."
>
> "The physical part of a relationship that brings a man and a woman closer by means of touch, cuddling, and kissing. Truly an important part of marriage!"
>
> "Sometimes physical pull, but other times it's my desire to take care of him."
>
> "Her sexy, sexy body."

God's View of Sex

The Bible says, "Honor marriage, and guard the sacredness of sexual intimacy between wife and husband. God draws a firm line against casual and elicit sex" (Heb. 13:4 Message). Now the first time I (Laura) heard this verse, I was a teenager in youth group. Of course our youth pastor was teaching us about not having sex outside of marriage. That makes sense. But when I recently read, "God draws a firm line against casual and elicit sex," I understood what *elicit sex* meant (sex outside of marriage or when you dabble in things like pornography), but the word *casual* really threw

89

> *The same can be said when we find our sex life boring. It's not our spouse; it's not our circumstances; it's our state of mind.*

me off. So I went to the dictionary and looked it up. I found: *careless, detached, unconcerned,* and *bored.* Hmm. Careless, detached, unconcerned, bored— could this be referring to sex within marriage? As I talk with couples all over the country, I hear this phrase time and time again: "I am bored with my marriage." "I am bored with my spouse." "I am bored with our sex."

We have a lot of experience with words like *bored* and *boring* because we have a teenager. It drives me (Jay) nuts when he says he is bored. I try to instill in my son that boredom is not what's happening or not happening around him; boredom is a state of mind.

The same can be said when we find our sex life boring. It's not our spouse; it's not our circumstances; it's our state of mind.

Listen to folks who have become bored with their sex life within their marriages.

"He's afraid of rejection."

"It runs in streaks. Sometimes we have to remind ourselves that it's important to be affectionate. At times we are too busy."

"I don't feel any need in the physical area, yet I am very physically affectionate."

"I know we don't 'do it' enough, and that's my fault. Either kids distract or I am too tired. I know this is a common excuse."

"As I get older I couldn't care less."

"I'm more hands-off because I've got a million other things to do . . . except at your marriage conferences on Mackinac Island."

"I gave up trying to initiate sex with my wife."

"He tries but I rarely give in. I tend to initiate so it's on my terms. This isn't particularly wonderful to him."

"I'm tired at the end of the day. I want to rest. I don't want any more hands touching me . . . even in the morning . . . I want time alone. I started to think of sex being good only in the arena of reproduction. When we wanted to get pregnant sex/intimacy was great."

"Over the years it has decreased because I am getting tired of being told 'no.'"

The Importance of Communication

Physical intimacy is the conscious desire to fulfill your spouse's sexual needs and the willingness to do so. We understand that due to age, medication, injury, or illness it isn't always possible to fulfill the needs of your spouse. And without question, communication in this area of marriage is very difficult. That being said, when healthy lines of communication about your sex life are open, growth in the relationship and physical intimacy will burgeon.

Defining *needs* versus *wants* in your sex life is critical to developing physical intimacy. For example, I *love* it when Laura puts on something sexy in the evening. Watching her prance around for a couple of hours before we go to bed really revs things up. With a teenager in the house, however, this is

> *Physical intimacy is the conscious desire to fulfill your spouse's sexual needs and the willingness to do so.*

rarely possible. So for me to tell Laura that I *need* her to dress that way would be unfair and unproductive in our efforts to build physical intimacy.

Over the years we have learned to communicate our true needs in the area of physical intimacy. I have let Laura know that there is a big difference for me between when she is "willing" and when she "wants to." In my twenties, her being "willing" was all I needed because, quite frankly, I was only concerned about my desires. As I've matured, I do not desire to have sex with Laura unless she really "wants to" as well. I know that for both of us, the experience of lovemaking will be so much more satisfying if she is truly in the mood.

When she is not in the mood, do I always react with maturity and understanding? Of course not! But I am learning how to respond and how to do those things the next day that will help her desire me.

A woman from our survey defines for us physical intimacy and how it is so much more than just physical:

> I read this in a book once, so it is not my personal definition, but I agree with it wholeheartedly. She wrote that the body and spirit make up the soul of a person and true physical intimacy is not just the connecting of two bodies but the joining of souls, both physical and spiritual union. Two shall be one flesh, literally speaking. God created physical union and Satan perverted it. It can be so much more if you can connect with someone on more than just a physical level.

What Motivates a Man?

Paul and Andrea are a cute couple. They were high school sweethearts who married after Andrea finished college.

Paul worked in Andrea's family business, and as they settled into married life God blessed them with two boys. Two very typical, normal, and energy-filled boys.

> *Defining **needs** versus **wants** in your sex life is critical to developing physical intimacy.*

A month or so ago Andrea joined a CD club. You know the kind: buy fifteen CDs for a dollar and agree to buy three more at regular price. When the CDs arrived, Paul and Andrea looked through the stack to confirm they received the CDs they ordered and to make sure there were no inappropriate covers. One particular CD featured a woman on the cover wearing a strapless dress. Paul and Andrea determined that the dress wasn't obscene or too scanty. They placed that particular CD in the middle of the pile and placed the pile on the stereo.

A couple of days later, Paul wandered into the family room to find their son Jack, age seven, sprawled on the floor intently staring at something Paul could not see. After watching Jack lay motionless for a few moments, Paul walked over and saw that he was staring at the cover of the CD that featured the woman in the strapless dress.

No one knows or understands this deep, inner desire men have for women, but the instinct starts young, and it is powerful. Some of my most vivid memories from early childhood are daydreams I had about one of my mom's friends. It wasn't dirty; it wasn't some Freudian fantasy. It was just me thinking about that pretty woman. It's instinctual.

Here are some typical answers from our survey regarding what motivates a man for physical intimacy.

"Everything!"
"Breathing!"

"Physical touch."

"Impulse."

"Thinking about her, looking at her, sleeping children—pretty much anything can motivate me if it relates to her. Heck, this question motivates me."

What Motivates a Woman?

Motivate is an interesting word. The dictionary defines it this way: "to move, to cause to act, to provide with a motive." So what motivates a woman to be physically intimate with her husband? I (Laura) personally like this answer from a woman who took our survey: "A lot of sleep and a vacation."

In talking with women across the country and in reading the surveys, I have found it interesting that most say an uncluttered mind is the greatest asset to physical intimacy. So the answer is easy: what motivates a woman is an empty brain. So men, if you want a wife who will have sex with you every day, marry an airhead! Seriously, though, make sure your wife's mental checklist is clear. Gentlemen, you can't unclutter your wife's mind. And every woman's mental checklist will look different. For example, Laura can go to bed with dirty dishes in the sink, but she can't even think about being romantic unless she is confident both kids are sound asleep. Therefore the key, guys, is to understand and be sensitive to *your* wife's mental checklist.

I (Laura) found the following answers from our survey interesting pertaining to what motivates a woman:

> *An uncluttered mind is the greatest asset to physical intimacy.*

"Age has made it better."

"Keeping the peace."

"Mental touch (words, eye contact, etc.)."

"Hearing Jay say at the Celebrate conference that men need sex about every seventy-two hours."

"My husband does the most (initiates). I try to consciously initiate more, but he often beats me to it—I can't keep up with him."

"We were virgins when we got married, so it has changed a lot and just seems to get better and better."

"Generally the fact that I know he needs it . . . once I've made the decision to be intimate, then most of the time I am interested in intimacy as well. But I definitely don't need physical intimacy the way he does, and I'm referring to holding hands, touching, kissing just as much or more than sex."

Let the Sparks Fly

In order to keep boredom from creeping into your sex life, we are going to challenge you with two very powerful words: *passionate* and *provocative*. We can improve our physical intimacy if we men learn to be more passionate and if women learn to be more provocative.

Passionate

Gentlemen, we must become *passionate*. Now some of you are thinking, *What do you mean, Jay? Like a soap opera thing?* Not really. Let's look at some words that help define *passionate*: *adoring, zealous, enthusiastic, eager, devoted, dedicated,* and *committed.* Most women would love to be with a man who is those things.

Men sometimes think they don't know much about passion, but we are all passionate about something. For instance, I am a passionate golfer. If my friend calls me up and says, "Jay, I've got an 8 a.m. tee time at your favorite golf course in northern Michigan," I think, *Okay, that's two hours away. That means I have to leave at six o'clock, but I want to get there and hit balls. That's 5:30. Oh, and I need some cushion time, that's 5:00. I also need to get up and take a shower, so that's 4:30 in the blessed a.m.! I'm there, buddy!*

What are you passionate about? Hunting? Fishing? Cars? Woodworking? Camping? Whatever the hobby, we know a lot about passion.

When are we passionate about our spouses? We are passionate about our spouses when we are eager and enthusiastic to be with them, devoted, dedicated, and committed to them. Gentlemen, if you start thinking in those terms about your spouse, you will unlock the woman of your dreams. She will see how much you care for her, and physical intimacy will grow.

Mike and Dee have been married for nineteen years and have three lovely daughters. Mike called me one day in the middle of March to enlist my help in a plan he was putting together for one of our Celebrate Your Marriage conferences in May. Mike had decided he was going to "kidnap" Dee and take her away for a romantic time on Mackinac Island.

Weekly, over the next two months, Mike would in one way or other drop hints of the wonderful adventure he had planned. Flowers delivered with a note saying, "I'm swept away with you!" A new dress purchased with the message "Just in case you need it!" You get the picture.

For two months all of these "hints" were building to a climax for the day of the "kidnapping." Further, all the hints made for two months of fun, romance, and yes, physical intimacy. Mike planned to work at romance, then worked the plan of romance and reaped the benefits of his passion!

Provocative

Ladies, we have to change our state of mind so we can become *provocative* in our marriage. Now some of you are thinking, *Laura, I can't do that. I'm a good girl, and that's a bad word.* Well if you look up *provocative* in the dictionary, you will find it means "inspiring, motivating, interesting, exciting, refreshing, energizing, and rousing." To be provocative is to provoke. To provoke means to arouse, stir up, excite, stimulate. There is nothing wrong or sinful about any of the words on this list.

You can become provocative for your spouse within your marriage. Your husband wants you to excite him, to stimulate him. I get so tickled, and exasperated, with Christian women who forget that God created sex! He created us to enjoy each other. God desires that you and your husband have a wonderful, satisfying sex life.

Here are some great examples of what it means to be provocative:

> "Since the age of thirty-five my libido has increased, and this made things much more fulfilling for both of us!"
>
> "Age has increased my desire. As I got older I found that I wanted physical intimacy more often. I think the kids being older and sleeping all night helped too."
>
> "It feels good when we are intimate. I enjoy the regular kisses, hugs, and walking hand in hand. I need to find more motivation to increase the level of sexual intimacy beyond the easy day-to-day encounters."
>
> "My wife is pleasant to our kids and pleasant to me. She spends a lot of time

God desires that you and your husband have a wonderful, satisfying sex life.

working out and has a physically attractive body. But it is not her physical shape that attracts me, it is her attitude of joy."

"I realize he needs me to initiate regularly so he knows it's important to me too."

"She wears something revealing or she says something with a little bit of zing to it."

"When we were first married, she would chase me around the house!"

There are many challenges for women who desire to deepen their physical intimacy with their husbands by being provocative. Following are two common issues for women in our culture.

Problem 1: Sex is dirty. If you grew up in the church, you were probably taught from an early age that sex is dirty, or at least that thought was implied. I have met many women who took a pledge as a teenager to wait until marriage for sex. Don't get me wrong, that is a wonderful pledge to take. What happens, though, is that along with the pledge comes a teaching, whether verbal or implied, that sex is dirty. Many of these women are now married and conflicted: "Now I am supposed to see sex as pleasurable, created by God. I can't just undo all those years of being taught sex was dirty!"

Debbie, a beautiful woman in her early thirties, came up to me after one of our conferences. She shared that she had been married just over seven years and their sex life had never been spectacular. As I began to ask questions I realized that Debbie had been a teenager who was very faithful to her youth group pledge and to her Lord. As a young girl, she decided that she wanted to remain pure until her wedding night. Her youth group offered an opportunity to make that commitment publicly, and Debbie did. She does not remember anyone ever saying the words, "Sex is dirty," but she does remember thinking and feeling that whenever it was a topic of conversation at home, church, or youth group. When she met her husband-to-be, they decided as a couple that they would remain sexually pure until their wedding night. They did.

On the night of their wedding, Debbie can remember going through the motions and then feeling very dirty afterwards. She was sure something was very wrong with her. As she came up to me that day, I saw a young woman, desperately in love with her husband, seeking to find an answer.

The answer required a change in her state of mind. For years Debbie's mind-set concerning sex was wrong. Sex is created by God for married couples to enjoy. Debbie had never understood that to be true because she had never been taught that as a teenager. We need to teach our young people that sex *outside of marriage* is a sin, and as such it is wrong and dirty. But at the same time we need to teach them that sex *within marriage* is dynamic, fun, and exciting. Teaching one without the other is setting any couple up for disappointment and potential disaster.

Problem 2: "To do" lists. Annie and Rob have been married for twenty-five years. Their firstborn has graduated from college and is soon to be married. Early in their marriage Annie and Rob faced some of the most difficult struggles any couple could face. The details aren't important; what is important are the little changes that made a big difference.

They spent the first ten years battling through their problems together. Through counseling and involvement in the church they began to take responsibility for their particular roles in their struggles. One of the simple yet powerful changes Annie talks about is the time her counselor made her go to bed for twenty-one straight days with dirty dishes in the sink. We know some of you women right now are cringing even at the thought. Annie did. You see, Annie is a type A, career-minded, self-confident woman who likes to get things done. As a result, if there were dishes in the sink or laundry to be done or a floor to be vacuumed, those duties took precedence over time with Rob. In fact Annie couldn't even think of being intimate with Rob unless everything on her "to do" list was done.

As a result, intimacy with Rob became just another "to do." Do the laundry. Do the dishes. Do intimacy with Rob. Many women reading this right now can relate; they are stuck in a cycle of habits that keep them from what they truly desire. Women want intimacy, passion, and romance in their marriage, and yes, your husband has a huge role in making that happen, but so do you!

The purpose behind the twenty-one days of trauma Annie's counselor prescribed her was to help her realize how insignificant dirty dishes are compared to the health and well-being of their marriage.

This second problem has never been a real issue in our marriage. I (Jay) guess I'm just lucky. Laura tells me I am because I married a middle child. Kevin Leman, in *The Birth Order Book*,[*] indicates that middle children are often good, reliable spouses because they are accustomed to making both older and younger siblings happy.

Laura has never struggled with the "it has to be done" syndrome; in fact, I am probably more prone to that mentality. Don't get me wrong, there are some nights when some

---

[*]Kevin Leman, *The Birth Order Book: Why You Are the Way You Are* (Grand Rapids: Revell, 2004).

task or issue is on Laura's mind and we are not going to so much as sit down to watch TV until it is crossed off her mental list. However, many are the nights when she'll look at me and say something like, "I filled the sink with water to let the dishes soak, and I'll finish them up in the morning." Or, "I know you need that shirt laundered by Friday, so I will do it tomorrow, just not tonight."

Do you know what that does for me? It communicates volumes; it tells me that she is doing something intentional for me—no, for us. It reflects the fact that she understands her side of the equation.

What do I do in response? I run upstairs, shower, shave, put on cologne and my finest sweatpants and T-shirt. Then I make sure the kids are sleeping or going to sleep really soon, pour her a diet Coke, get the crackers, and slice the cheese.

Desire Is a Decision

Earlier in this book we talked about the fact that for women intimacy is like a Crock-Pot; they take all day to cook. For men, intimacy is more like a microwave. This is the way God created us, and we cannot change that, but we can work with what we have. What this means, ladies, is not only that our husbands have to plug us in and let us cook all day long, but when they plug us in, we cannot unplug ourselves!

I (Laura) have learned over the years that while I have a billion other things on my mind during the day, I must have my husband on my mind as well. My mind is my greatest asset when it comes to my sex life with my husband.

When Jay first started traveling as a speaker, he was gone several days a week as well as the weekend. He usually returned home on a Sunday evening and wanted to be greeted at the door with a big, sloppy kiss. I, on the other hand, had been holding down the fort at home, taking care of kids every minute of every day. The second he walked in the door I was done! It was his turn to give a bath or read a bedtime story. And sex was the farthest thing from my mind.

Maybe your husband is home every night. Yet your day is still filled with meals, laundry, activities, bath time, bedtime, and tomorrow's plans!

I realized as Jay's schedule and my routine hampered our intimate life that I had to do some mental preparation. I had to anticipate his homecoming. I had to focus my mind halfway through his absence on the fact that when he returned home he would want sex! What I discovered was that the more I focused on that, the more I desired to give him a big, sloppy kiss when he stepped through that door. Desire is a decision. Many times we have to decide to "be in the mood."

In this quote from Debi, we see a woman who has made a cognitive decision to take time away from their kids and schedule in order to maintain a deeper level of physical intimacy:

> Having two kids and a busy life with crazy schedules makes it difficult to be together. However, we took measures to have "alone time" shortly before coming to the Celebrate Your Marriage conference this past May. It's only gotten better since the conference—it helped me realize how important it is to maintain physical intimacy even if I may feel too tired.

> *My mind is my greatest asset when it comes to my sex life with my husband.*

Susan had to retrain her mind. Her upbringing had predisposed her to negative images that she overcame in order to deepen her marriage relationship:

> *Desire is a decision. Many times we have to decide to "be in the mood."*

The area that has changed is more frequent intercourse. This has been brought on by honesty in our relationship, a conscious attempt by me to want to please my husband and obey God as well, and viewing sex differently. (It's okay to do it, and not only that—God expects me to do it often!) This is a huge change for a girl who has been taught all her life that sex is wrong—suddenly you get married and then it's okay and not a wrong thing and you are supposed to suddenly do it. (Needless to say, our wedding night years ago was . . . well . . . I think you get the picture.) Also, as my husband has grown spiritually, it has brought us closer together and sex is better than ever—as God intends it to be.

Practice What You Preach

One of our teachings that really tends to turn heads is that we believe sexual intercourse is one of the deepest forms of worshiping God. See, told you. Just so you don't think we are the only ones thinking this way, following is a survey response from a woman explaining a moment of deep spiritual intimacy with her husband: "Okay, don't be shocked, but I wish I could explain to newlyweds how good sex is when you bring God to bed with you—what I mean is to know that it is by God's design that you are married and God gave you (the married person) sex."

In Romans we read: "Therefore, I urge you, brothers, in view of God's mercy, to offer your bodies as living sacrifices, holy and pleasing to God—this is your spiritual act of worship" (Rom. 12:1). Worship is offering our bodies as unconditional sacrifices to a God we trust with our life. In marriage when we offer our bodies unconditionally to a spouse we trust with our love, we please God. Can we as husbands and wives have sex without bringing God to bed with us? Yes, but when we do we miss out on God's best for our physical intimacy.

Truly, in the purest form, lovemaking between a husband and a wife is the "offering of our bodies as living sacrifices" in order to bring our spouse pleasure. If we are followers of Christ, and we bring him to bed with us, then we are making love, which he created, and in turn giving him the glory, honor, and praise.

We have many friends who cringe at the thought of bringing Jesus to bed. We believe it is bred out of a cultural mind-set that still considers sex as dirty and naughty rather than a gift from God. God created sexual intimacy between a husband and a wife for our enjoyment and pleasure. He created it, and it is very good!

Mike and Linda understand that physical intimacy is sharing so much more than just their bodies. It is the sharing of Mike's entire person—physical, spiritual, mental, and emotional—with Linda. Intimacy is that sharing of our entire beings with another person. When we miss the mark and share only a part of who we are, it is like eating chocolate cake without the chocolate or the icing!

Don and Joann shared in our survey that physical intimacy starts for them long before the physical act. Having fun together or deep conversation is the foreplay in their relationship. Again, we see that the sharing of friendship and conversation (social and mental intimacy) is the beginning to physical intimacy.

Shari reported that since her husband has become a Christian he is much more concerned about her when it comes to physical intimacy. He has lost the selfishness that desires only his pleasure and is more attentive to her needs and pleasure. In Shari's comments we can see that spiritual intimacy plays a large role in the fulfillment of physical intimacy in a marriage relationship.

> *God created sexual intimacy between a husband and a wife for our enjoyment and pleasure. He created it, and it is very good!*

When I (Jay) was sixteen, my mom and I were doing dishes together after dinner. That in and of itself was a miracle! I knew that my mom and dad were going through a stretch of rough water. As we were washing dishes, I asked my mother if she and Dad were going to get a divorce. Almost before the words got out of my mouth, my mother had swatted me upside the head with the dish towel! She responded to my question in these words, "Jay, if there is one thing I know, it is that your father and I will never get a divorce. You see, son, your dad loves Jesus even more than he loves me."

What a powerful statement! When we love Jesus and love our spouse, physical intimacy will become more about the other person than it is about our desires or needs.

Donna shares in her survey response that she is most responsive to Ron, her husband, in the physical realm when she feels emotionally connected to him. This connection involves respect from him, relaxation, laughter, and verbal communication. She shared that even when she begins the evening not feeling "in the mood," this emotional connection can change her mood.

Donna's response points us back to "desire is a decision." In that section of the book, I (Laura) was talking mainly to women about putting aside all the distractions of the day and deciding to desire your husband. Jay says that my being "willing to" is not the same as "wanting to." I agree. Men need to understand that women will "want to" more if they feel that emotional connection to their husbands. The respect, the conversation, the laughter may take some effort on their part to get the "want to" started!

As we can see in all these examples from our survey, all five facets of intimacy are so entwined that you cannot have one without the other and experience all that God intended for marriage.

Attractors and Detractors

As we have seen in the previous section, physical intimacy is much more than the sexual act. The attractors involve all five facets of intimacy. Some spouses are attracted by the friendship, others by conversation, still others by the emotional connection, and some by their faith.

In large part, for most couples we surveyed, physical intimacy has grown in their marriage. What began as just physical has become deeper in all levels of intimacy. Overwhelmingly, the most common attractor to physical intimacy was not the outward appearance of a spouse but the emotional connection between a couple. However, outward circumstances were also an attractor. For example, dating, displays of affection, working together—all are outward circumstances that lead to the connection that in turn leads to physical intimacy.

Health issues, busyness, and lack of understanding were the most common detractors. As we age, our bodies may begin to need medications that can affect our sex drives. That is understood. However, physical intimacy is so much more, as we have seen, than having sexual intercourse. I (Laura) believe that as we age we can still have sexual intimacy in spite of what our bodies may be telling us!

Other health issues, illness, and disease are unfortunate realities of living in a fallen world. I know for some it is only for a season of their marriage and for others it is a lifetime.

My father was diabetic and was crippled in his legs because of polio he had contracted at a young age. During my lifetime he had four heart attacks and three strokes. His illness was not just a season but a lifetime, and the life of my parents' marriage. Was it easy? Absolutely not. There was stress, frustration, and anxiety. Yet I know beyond a shadow of a doubt that my parents loved each other. The physical act may have been difficult (however they did produce four children!), yet the intimacy was still there.

Busyness and lack of understanding were also high on the list of detractors to physical intimacy. We as a couple have to make our marriage a priority. (We will address this later in the book.) Unfortunately, we make the choice, consciously or unconsciously, to allow busyness to creep into our lives.

The two most powerful words we can learn to say are *yes* and *no*. As a couple we have to decide what we are going to say *yes* to and what we are going to say *no* to. We have to choose to eliminate the busyness in our lives for the sake of our marriage.

Lack of understanding is a result of an inward, *me* focus as opposed to an outward, *other* focus. Laura is what I (Laura) am all about! I am mostly concerned with my desires, my wants, and my needs, which can cripple our

> *We have to choose to eliminate the busyness in our lives for the sake of our marriage.*

physical intimacy. It takes effort on a daily basis to put *me* aside. I don't do it well, and I don't do it all the time. Yet I try! Jay sees that I try and respects that and is grateful. I may not get it right all the time, but the effort is seen and appreciated.

Questions for Reflection and Discussion

1. From your perspective, rate the level of physical intimacy in your marriage on a scale of 1 to 10.
2. In what ways do you think you and your spouse succeed at being passionate and provocative?
3. In what ways do you need to improve being passionate and provocative?
4. What detractors to physical intimacy can you identify in your marriage?
5. What attractors to physical intimacy can you identify in your marriage?
6. What is one way you can improve your physical intimacy over the next twenty-one days?

8

Spiritual Intimacy

The Eternal Flame

We all need to be spiritually intimate if we are going to be intimate with our spouses because that is the foundation of all the other facets of intimacy. We don't know where you are in your spiritual life. Some readers may not have a relationship with Jesus, and we want to meet you where you are. But hopefully you will agree with us that all humans are not only physical but also spiritual beings.

When she was five years old our daughter understood that she is a spiritual being, that there's something bigger out there. We remember one particular church service when our pastor was preaching a powerful sermon on the fact that in the cosmos we are nothing but dust. We're insignificant in the grand scheme of the universe. At the end of his sermon, he raised his hands and prayed, "Oh Lord, even though we are but dust. . . ." Gracie had been listening carefully that day and had her head bowed. As soon as those words came out of his mouth, her head snapped up and she asked, "Daddy, what's butt dust?"

The Simplest Form of Church

Most would agree that church is the physical presence of Christ on earth. We, as husband and wife, therefore are the church here on earth. (We firmly believe this *does not* mean we use this as an excuse to refrain from corporate worship with other believers.) We can become spiritually intimate when we understand what God has for our marriage.

Listen to the words of Jesus:

> I tell you the truth, whatever you bind on earth will be bound in heaven, and whatever you loose on earth will be loosed in heaven. Again, I tell you that if two of you on earth agree about anything you ask, it will be done for you by my Father in heaven. For when two or three come together in my name, there I am with them.
>
> Matthew 18:18–20

What do these verses have to say to married couples? One way to read them is like this: If you and your spouse agree upon anything, our Father in heaven will hear you. If you ask for it in Jesus's name, in accordance with his will, he will grant it to you in your marriage. Also, if you loose anything in your marriage—destructive habits, things that you know are not healthy for your relationship—and say, "Lord, we want those out of our lives if it's in accordance with your will," they will be loosed for you.

Laura's Financial Wizardry

As Jay mentioned earlier, he figured out right away that I was no financial genius! When we met I was sure that the ATM machine could keep track of my debits and magically record them in my checkbook! Thus, six weeks after graduating from college I was overdrawn—fourteen bounced checks overdrawn.

So Jay's lifelong challenge became to help me at least know how to balance a checkbook and pay bills in case the day ever came when I had to do it alone. After about nine years of training he decided that I could at last be in charge of the family finances. It was an experiment that lasted one year.

Unbeknownst to Jay, I was failing fast. But I was so determined to fix it, I refused to ask for help. So I sank deeper and deeper into financial trouble. At the same time, unbeknownst to me, Jay was planning ahead to give me a special gift for our ten-year anniversary. Whenever he went out to speak, he gave me the honorarium to deposit but kept the travel expense reimbursement checks and deposited them in a secret savings account.

On our tenth anniversary, the truth both of us had been hiding came to light. Jay gave me a check and said I could spend it any way I desired. I bawled! Then I told him about my financial troubles! The miracle of the whole thing was that the amount Jay had saved matched to a penny the debt I had incurred in my unwillingness to ask for help.

God's grace sprouted two legs and walked into my life in the form of my husband. Here he had saved for an entire year to give me a check, and I had been too proud to ask for help in my weakness.

We chose to "loose" this issue in our marriage. Jay forgave me. We looked at our budget, made some sacrifical alterations (e.g., not dining out), and paid off the debt I had incurred. We then committed our future financial decisions to the Lord.

Defining Spiritual Intimacy

If one were to draw a picture of deepening spiritual intimacy, it would look like a triangle. As two people in a marriage grow closer to the Lord, they cannot help but grow closer to each other.

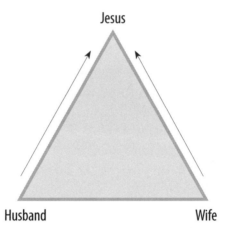

The process of becoming one spiritually occurs when a husband and wife mutually commit to being conformed to the image of Christ. Two amazing transformations happen in this process. First, I become more of the person God intended me to be. Second, I become more of the person my spouse truly needs me to be.

Here is how others define spiritual intimacy:

"Spiritual intimacy involves loving God and accepting Jesus as our Savior. Living with JOY: Jesus, Others, You."

"I think that when we are intimate with God, it creates a 'something' in us to love each other more, without saying a word or touching each other. It's all from the soul."

"Being able to connect to one another through Christ."

"We go to church and discuss our thoughts on the sermon; we discuss current issues and how they affect our lives spiritually and how we may differ in opinion."

> *The process of becoming one spiritually occurs when a husband and wife mutually commit to being conformed to the image of Christ.*

"When two or more people are 'in tune' with the Holy Spirit at the same time."

"For Joy and me, it is being able to sit down together and go through a particular event (either in Scripture or in our lives) and know that we are on the same page, that God is in control."

"I think spiritual intimacy with God can be summed up in two words: *trust* and *obey*."

"Having a personal, 24/7 relationship with God. Not just turning to him when things go wrong or you need him to help you out."

"When we have the same mind while praying together and agree together about issues or respect the other for his or her input during prayer."

"The closeness that you feel as a unit that includes the two of you with your foundation being Christ."

"Respecting the other for their input during prayer."

"Where you feel unified by the Holy Spirit. That the Spirit is helping you to grow in your walk with the Lord together. You share the same spiritual goals and values. Where you can love your spouse more selflessly because the Spirit helps you to give beyond your selfishness."

"We are emotionally and mentally as well as physically pure to each other. No outside influences, fantasies, and so forth. We talk about what a wonderful gift God has given us and how much we cherish it."

"I think that it has many levels, one of which is a common belief in our Savior Jesus Christ. I think when you can share your deep love for the Savior and the work he has done in your life and have those feelings reciprocated by your spouse that to me would be true spiritual intimacy."

"Where you feel unified by the Holy Spirit. That the Spirit is helping you to grow in your walk with the Lord together. You share the same spiritual goals and values."

Spiritual Intimacy Impacts Daily Life

Robin and Jonathan were like any other couple when they first got married. Adjusting to the challenges of marriage made for good days and bad. Jonathan had been raised in a home where financial management was an important part of being a steward of all God had given them. Robin was more than willing to defer to Jonathan's plans.

Early in their marriage they put forth a financial plan and literally dedicated that plan to the Lord. Jonathan and Robin have never been what the world would call rich. Jonathan has a good job as an accountant, but Robin does not work outside the home. Together they made three simple commitments:

1. The Lord gets paid first.
2. Our savings gets paid second.
3. We will budget our lifestyle based on what's left over.

In nearly twenty years of marriage Jonathan and Robin have worked this plan. They don't buy anything on credit, and their house is paid off. When asked about their financial success, they cheerfully say it was a spiritual decision that had real-world implications.

> *Early in their marriage they put forth a financial plan and literally dedicated that plan to the Lord.*

Opening the Rooms of Your Heart

God has offered us power, and yet so often we fail to use it. Those of us who know Jesus have the power that created the universe living within our hearts. This reminds me of when my friend Russ put a furnace into my home a few months ago. Russ is a plumbing and heating contractor, and his guys installed a brand-new furnace. He was talking to me about BTUs and CFMs and all this stuff I didn't understand. The conversation went like this:

I asked, "Russ, will it heat my house?"

He declared, "Oh boy, this is a powerful furnace. Feel the heat coming off of this right now."

I replied, "Yeah, but will it heat everything?"

He exclaimed, "Oh yeah, it will push a lot of heat."

I responded, "But Russ, will it cover every room of my house?"

He finally replied, "Only if you go through every room in your house and you open those little vents. Otherwise, no, it can't do its work."

For those of us who have asked the Lord Jesus Christ to live within us, the power of the Holy Spirit is available to us. Jesus is waiting to warm every aspect of your marriage, every aspect of your heart. We must pray and open the vents in every room and allow him to invade every aspect of our marriage, making us mentally, socially, emotionally, physically, and spiritually intimate.

Confession Is Good for the Soul

We believe that spiritual intimacy begins with a simple yet powerful biblical concept. We must confess our sins and our weaknesses.

> He who conceals his sins does not prosper, but whoever *confesses* and renounces them finds mercy.
>
> Proverbs 28:13 (emphasis added)

> Therefore *confess* your sins to each other and pray for each other so that you may be healed. The prayer of a righteous man is powerful and effective.
>
> James 5:16 (emphasis added)

> If we *confess* our sins, he is faithful and just and will forgive us our sins and purify us from all unrighteousness.
>
> 1 John 1:9 (emphasis added)

Clearly, there is spiritual power beyond our understanding when we confess. In marriage there are pivotal moments of confession. I (Laura) struggle with being selfish. I don't know why. Perhaps it is because I am the third of four kids and thought I needed to fight for equal opportunity. This created in me a "tit for tat, this for that" mentality in our marriage, which came to a head with the birth of our son, Torrey.

I was going to have to be home more and do ministry less, and I thought I was going to have to sit back and watch Jay have all the fun in life! My selfish nature cropped up and I found myself being irritable, bitter, and resentful. I frequently launched into unexpected tirades. My loving husband asked what he could do to help. Then I realized there was nothing he could do to help me until I confessed that the root of my problem was my selfishness. The day I did that it was as if a cloud was lifted from my life.

We must pray and open the vents in every room and allow him to invade every aspect of our marriage, making us mentally, socially, emotionally, physically, and spiritually intimate.

In marriage there are also recurring moments of confession. I (Jay) am a typical firstborn, type A personality. I could easily live by the moniker, "It's my way or the highway." Early in our marriage, I demanded much from my bride without giving her grace to mature in her role as a wife. Unfortunately my demanding ways continue to crop up on a recurring basis: "Why is the laundry piled up?" "What are your plans for cooking dinner?" "Is this house ever going to get cleaned?" All the while I am failing to remember that Laura works full-time as an author and speaker as well as needing to give her time, love, and attention to our two beautiful children. I have to daily remind myself to ask her forgiveness for my insensitive and demanding ways.

Confession is the beginning of unleashing the Holy Spirit's power in every aspect of our life. To whom do we confess? Obviously, we are called to confess our sins to the Lord. Further, God has given you a partner in the person of your spouse with whom to share the innermost joys, struggles, and challenges of your life. It will not be easy, but the benefits will be immeasurable.

We Just Don't Understand!

In our survey we asked many different questions about each of the five facets of intimacy that we have covered to this point: social, mental, emotional, physical, and spiritual. We also asked respondents to rate where their marriage is in relation to each facet on a scale from 1 to 10 (see appendix A to take the survey). What amazed us was that many people rated their marriage low (1 to 3) on all of the facets except spiritual intimacy, and then they gave their marriage a 10.

Here is the thing. You cannot be intimate spiritually without it radically improving your intimacy in the other facets of your marriage. This is where well-meaning people can totally misunderstand what intimacy in marriage is all about. It goes beyond what our minds have ever tried to comprehend before. Spiritual intimacy is so much more than attending church together and praying together. It is the meshing of all the facets—social, mental, emotional, physical, and spiritual—in a way that intertwines you and your spouse heart, mind, body, and soul.

You cannot be intimate spiritually without it radically improving your intimacy in the other facets of your marriage.

If in fact you are becoming more like Christ every day, you will become more aware of and in tune with the needs, wants, and desires of your spouse. As a selfless follower of Jesus, you will desire to meet those needs, wants, and desires in a deep and real way as an offering to

Christ and an example of *his* power to the world. So let us be frank here. If you are rating your marriage high in spiritual intimacy and low in the other areas, you might want to take a closer look at what is really taking place spiritually, in your own life and in your marriage. Are you really experiencing the abundant life Christ speaks of, or are you merely going through the motions of an "institutional" relationship with Jesus?

Through God's Power

God's power is here and now. He wants us to go through our marriage and open up all the vents in our lives—the vents of social, emotional, physical, and spiritual intimacy. As we open those vents and use his power, we are laying our marriage down before him. We're saying, "You know, it's not my desires, not my expectations, not my needs. Lord, take this marriage, take my spouse and make him or her into the partner I need, and Lord, take me and make me into the partner that my spouse needs." As you do that, the Lord will fashion your marriage into a beautiful expression of love and unity.

May your life be a life of unbelievable joy. Jesus Christ said, "I have come that they may have life, and have it to the full" (John 10:10). We want to encourage you to learn to dance with each other so that as you go through life you dance along and celebrate every day.

Attractors to Spiritual Intimacy

The obvious attractor for couples when it comes to spiritual intimacy is a shared faith. Yet the responses from our survey show not only a shared faith but serving together, worshiping together, and praying together as huge attractors to spiritual intimacy.

All too often married couples may believe that simply sharing the same belief system is intimacy when, in actuality, acting out this shared belief system is how spiritual intimacy grows. As a college student I (Laura) had great hope for the future! I was looking forward to becoming a youth minister (that was my course of study), marrying a man, raising a family—all the hopes that a young woman has at that age. In a marriage and family course in which I enrolled, I distinctly remember advice the professor gave us. She said decide your master first—whom will you serve. Second, decide your mission—what it is that you want to do with your life. Last, decide your mate—with whom will you choose to spend your life.

This made perfect sense to me because I knew that I had a relationship with Jesus Christ—he was my Master. I knew I wanted to be a youth minister—that was my mission. The mate was the last decision to make.

I truly think that in our Western mind-set we get this all backwards. Many times we decide whom we will marry before we have decided whom we will serve and what our mission is in life. Therefore, after we marry we often find that our spouse does not have the same priorities, and in fact, his or her choices may be in conflict with ours.

One huge attractor for me when I met Jay was that he had chosen his Master, and his mission was in sync with mine. We knew almost right away that ministering together was what we desired in our marriage.

> *Decide your master first. . . . Second, decide your mission. . . . Last, decide your mate.*

Another spiritual attractor frequently mentioned was

praying together. Prayer is probably one of the most vulnerable, intimate actions a couple can do together. You are opening up your heart and soul before not only your spouse but also the God of creation! This is

> *Prayer is probably one of the most vulnerable, intimate actions a couple can do together.*

why this is difficult for many couples. I (Jay) have actually heard couples comment that it is easier to undress in front of each other than it is to pray together.

We have a small group of friends (couples) who meet once a week for accountability and prayer. At our meeting around Valentine's Day, I (Jay) was facilitating the group that evening, and I decided that we should spend time in directed prayer. I led an exercise of each one praying specifically for his or her spouse. The prayer was to be one of thankfulness for the spouse. It was not an easy task, but each person prayed thanking God for his or her spouse. The interesting thing I noticed afterward was how cuddly everyone was with their spouses! Prayer is an intimate act that is a great attractor to spiritual intimacy.

Detractors to Spiritual Intimacy

On the flip side of these attractors are the natural opposites, which are detractors: feeling disconnected spiritually from a spouse. Many survey respondents used the words *disconnected, separateness,* and *lack of togetherness.* As we studied our surveys we found three basic issues in this feeling of disconnectedness: a spouse who is overly involved in church activities and has no time, spouses who are both believers but do not share service or prayer (as discussed above), or the spouse who does not share the same faith.

121

A Christian married to a non-Christian will find it very difficult to be spiritually intimate. We have watched many friends in this situation. For most people it is a constant challenge to love as Christ loves. Those who succeed in this situation stay in the marriage and continue to pray for their spouse, love their spouse in a Christlike manner, and remain committed to their relationship with both God and their spouse.

The other two most common detractors are an overly involved spouse and a spouse who does not share in serving. These two seem to go hand in hand. A lesson that has helped our marriage immensely is one Jay and I both had to learn. Many times, one of us has to say *no* to something that is a good thing in order to say *yes* to something great.

Related to this, we believe one of the biggest detriments to a marriage is the church's separation of ministry areas. For example, walk into almost any church in America and you will find listed in their directory women's ministries, men's ministries, singles' ministries, children's ministries, and youth ministries. It is rare in America today to find a church that has a specific marriage and family minister, let alone a directed marriage ministry. On a given Sunday, families walk into church and immediately go their separate ways. Church committees rarely have people serve as couples. Women's retreats, men's retreats, events, and so on all separate couples. This is a direct reason we have established our Marriage Champion program. (For more information on Marriage Champions see appendix C.)

We are not saying that a couple should never be apart and attend events separately or even do activities with friends. What we are saying is that the focus of church should do more to bring couples together, giving couples the opportunities to serve together.

At one point in our marriage, I (Laura) was involved in two women's Bible studies, taught aerobics for a group of women, served on the women's ministry committee, and attended a mother's morning out group. Did I have time for Jay? Only at night, and that was if I was not too tired from all my activities! Are these all good activities to be involved in? YES! But I had to say *no* to some of these good activities in order to say *yes* to something better—my husband and our marriage.

Questions for Reflection and Discussion

1. From your perspective, rate the level of spiritual intimacy in your marriage on a scale of 1 to 10.
2. Identify how you and your spouse express yourself spiritually.
3. Identify the common spiritual values that you share as a couple.
4. Explain your relationship, as well as your spouse's, to Jesus Christ.
5. What detractors to spiritual intimacy can you identify in your marriage?
6. What attractors to spiritual intimacy can you identify in your marriage?
7. How can you deepen your walk with Christ over the next twenty-one days?

PART TWO

BRINGING THE FACETS OF INTIMACY TOGETHER

9

Lose Yourself

Tending the Fire

Now you may be wondering, "How is this 'being one' going to impact my marriage?" This may sound silly, but the reality is that being one impacts every aspect of our lives. The reason it impacts every aspect of life comes from the first action we must practice to be one: losing ourselves.

The Butter Putter

For me (Jay), one of the places it's hard to lose myself is when it comes to my golf game. I love golf, but normally if I'm going to invest—and that's the word I like to use—in a golf club, I will talk to Laura about it. We make our budgetary decisions together, even when it comes to some of the smaller stuff, because we believe that is what it means to practice being one.

As I said, I am a chaplain for the PGA, serving primarily on the Nationwide Tour. In that capacity I was asked to speak at the Detroit Golf Show, which is the second largest golf show in America. After speaking at a prayer breakfast there, my friends and I walked around the booths looking at different clubs. We came to an exhibit where they were selling putters. Putters—the most precious club in the bag. It is the club that can cure all evil things that happen in a golf game—slices, hooks, and duffs.

I began to stroke golf balls with this putter. It was so smooth. Smooth like butter—I call it my butter putter. It was mesmerizing, tantalizing. Without realizing it, I reached into my wallet and handed the guy $140 for that putter. I've never spent that much on any club in my bag, but badabing badaboom, I bought the putter.

Driving home, I was so excited. I'm going to tell Laura about the putter. I can't wait for Laura to see my new putter . . . uh . . . er . . . oh NO, I forgot to talk to Laura about the putter. YIKES!

I must admit that if I had discussed it with her before, asking, "Honey, I'm thinking about buying a putter or some other club. Is that okay?" she would have said, "You know, let's look at the budget. Okay, you can spend $50." I had overstepped our agreement about spending without consulting her. Self had sneaked in, and instead of losing self, I embraced self.

Making Decisions Together

I (Laura) am a shopper. Here is how being one has affected me. My mode of operation when my daughter has a dance lesson or piano lesson is to wander through Wal-Mart. I am just going to see what they have on the shelves. I don't really need anything when I go in, but when I come out, I have a whole cart full of things that suddenly I needed when I was in the store. I go home and exclaim, "Look at all these things I needed at Wal-Mart."

When we make the conscious choice to communicate about decisions and come to conclusions together, we become one.

When Jay and I began to talk about being one and how it affects not only the physical area but all the different areas of our life together, I realized my desire to shop for needless items was hindering our ability to be one. So I made a "Wal-Mart plan." I decided that before I go to Wal-Mart I have to tell Jay what I'm going to buy. I must have a list.

Some of you are probably uncomfortable with the idea of losing yourself to become one. You may be thinking, "I don't like this. What do you mean, lose myself? I'm not a child; I can make decisions on my own!" You are right. We all can. However, when we make the conscious choice to communicate about decisions and come to conclusions together, we become one. So let's look to Scripture to see how we go about losing the self.

Philippians 2:3 talks about an attitude we should have: "Do nothing out of selfish ambition or vain conceit." Let's stop right there for a moment. Each one of us could benefit from typing up that sentence and putting it on our refrigerator. It is a great sentence by which to live the rest of our lives—especially in marriage, where it can be so difficult.

> Do nothing out of selfish ambition or vain conceit, but in humility consider others better than yourselves. Each of

you should look not to your own interests, but also to the interests of others. Your attitude should be the same as that of Christ Jesus: Who, being in very nature God, did not consider equality with God something to be grasped, but made himself nothing, taking the very nature of a servant, being made in human likeness. And being found in appearance as a man, he humbled himself and became obedient to death—even death on a cross.

Philippians 2:3–8

This passage of Scripture says that Jesus made himself nothing. What does that mean? He was found in *human* likeness. So what does that say about us? We're all big fat zeros. In the broad scope of the universe and eternity, we are dust. I think the writers of the Scripture and God himself as he was inspiring them had to have a chuckle or two. Why? Because as humans we tend to think so highly of ourselves when in the broad scope of time and space we are nothing.

The Role of Self-Esteem

Self-esteem is something that everybody struggles with at one level or another because of what we see on TV and in magazines. But we need to remember this: Throughout the creation story, when God created something he proclaimed, "That's good." He created the earth and the sun and proclaimed, "That's good." After separating the sea and the land, he declared, "That's good." When he designed the birds of the air and the fish of the sea, he announced, "That's good." When he made the zebra, the giraffe, and the duck-billed platypus, he said, "Okay, they're strange but good." But do you know what God said when he made us?

After he made humans, after he made you, he said, "That is very good."

I've got to tell you, I'm a lot like you. I (Jay) wake up in the morning, look in the mirror, and think, *That ain't very good.* I've got more down here on my waistline than I want, less up here on my hairline than I want. Can you relate?

We all have poor self-image because of the world in which we live. Burger King says, "Have it *your* way." Ladies, you use L'Oreal because, *"I'm* worth it." There's even a magazine called *Self*, for crying out loud. Most of us spend the first twenty to twenty-five years of our life being told, "It's all about you." We're told: "You've got to get *your* education." "You've got to find *your* job." "You have to make *your* career." You're even looking for what? *Your* spouse, and he or she is going to fulfill every one of . . . *your* needs. Why? Because it's all about *you*, baby!

In reality, if we're going to be one, we have to realize that when we stood at that altar and said "I do," we relinquished every right to self. Every right. So the question is this: Are you going to lose yourself? Are you going to lose yourself for the sake of the marriage? You are not losing to your spouse but to the marriage. You are losing yourself so that you can be one and have a life that is built around exactly what God wants for you and your marriage.

"Put to death, therefore, whatever belongs to your earthly nature" (Col. 3:5). Simply put, we're talking about the ego side of self; the *self*ishness, *self*-centeredness that we all can display. In *no way* would we ever contend that you should quit being the unique individual God made you to be. You

> *Are you going to lose yourself for the sake of the marriage?*

131

have gifts and personality that need to shine. But we have to put our selfish tendencies and desires aside for the sake of the marriage.

The following diagrams illustrate how we believe this comes together.

Some people will teach you that I am here, my spouse is there, and then there is a third entity called the marriage. Nowhere in Scripture do we find anything that supports this idea.

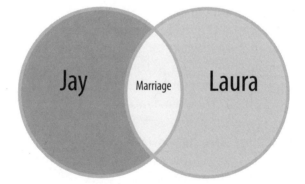

We believe that the more you lose yourself in marriage, the more the marriage grows. As that marriage grows, you will begin to understand exactly how God wants you and your spouse to live.

At some point you will become not you and your spouse who are married, but the marriage of you and your spouse. This is significantly different.

In the final illustration, the three circles have become one. Some might look at this and think we are asking couples to completely give up their individuality. In reality, however, what we are saying is to be completely who you are but do so in the context of growing the marriage.

Let me give you an illustration of how this works. I (Jay) married a sleeper. Laura loves sleep, will sleep anytime she can, and sleep she will! Laura is not a lazy person; she just loves to sleep. And if I wake her up while she's sleeping? Well, let's just say that it is a very bad thing.

When we get the kids up for school each day, we tag team it. Laura planned it this way: "Jay, we've got to wake the kids up at 6:40 if they're going to make it to school on time. I'll set the alarm, and I will roll out at 6:40 and start them moving. Then I'll go downstairs and make breakfast and pack their lunches. Now, what I want you to do is to sleep another ten to fifteen minutes and then make sure the kids are moving along."

Contrast that to her nature (as a sleeper). Her nature would say, "Jay, when the alarm goes off, I'm going to kick you out of bed. You get the kids rolling because I'm going to sleep an extra ten to fifteen minutes." But no, she denies her desire to sleep, which is part of her very nature. Laura jokes that she is afraid of how the kids will be dressed if I get them up first. I would not notice that plaids and stripes do not match! But in reality she is giving up sleep, losing that part of herself, for the sake of our marriage and family.

The Big Book of Right

I (Laura) have found that a lot of us view marriage as a competition. Who works more? Who cooks more meals? Who puts more gas in the car? Who does the most house-cleaning? Who is right more often? Who is wrong more often? We keep a little scorecard, and this approach is deadly to intimacy.

I am the third of four kids, so growing up I was never right. There were always four other people ahead of me: Mom, Dad, Sandy, and Greg. Those people were always going to be right before me, so I decided that when I got married, that would be my time to be right. I decided I was going to keep track of it so I could prove how right I am and how often I am right. So I planned to buy a big old notebook and put a label on the front that read, "Laura's Big Book of Right." It was going to be a *big* notebook. Okay, so I didn't actually buy a notebook, but I had reserved an entire section of my brain to keep score.

> *Marriage is about being one, not about being right. God didn't call us to be right; he called us to be one.*

I had plans for being right all the time. Do you want to know how many times I've been right? Absolutely none. Do you know why? Because marriage is not about who is right and who is wrong, who works more and who works less, who puts more gas in the car, who takes care of the kids more often. Marriage is about being one, not about being right. God didn't call us to be right; he called us to be one.

In Mark 10:6–8, we read, "But at the beginning of creation, God 'made them male and female.' 'For this reason a man will leave his father and mother and be united to his wife, and the two will become one flesh.' So they are no longer two, but one." The phrase "one flesh" in Greek is *sarka mian*, which translates the Hebrew *basar echad*, quoted here from Genesis 2:24. I just love that expression *basar echad* because it means "one flesh, one body, one person." The wording indicates that the relationship between a man and a woman as husband and wife is not only one of monogamy and marital consummation but also of complete unity.* What's equally fascinating is the "cleave, cling, join, be united" part that comes just before in Genesis 2:24,

---

*N. P. Bratsiotis, "בָּשָׂר *bāśār*," *Theological Dictionary of the Old Testament*, vol. 2, rev. ed., ed. G. Johannes Botterweck and Helmer Ringgren, trans. John T. Willis (Grand Rapids: Eerdmans, 1977), 328.

> *We simply had to give them up in order to do what was best for our marriage, what was best in order to make us one.*

which conveys the idea of being glued together in a permanent bond.

The Yes-Woman and the No-Man

Soon after we moved to Alma to work for Youth for Christ, Laura and I had our roles at church down pat. She was the yes-woman, saying *yes* to everything that came along. At one point Laura was on the drama team, in the cookie ministry, a greeter, on the youth board, on a hospitality team, a nursery volunteer, and, last but not least, an aerobics teacher at our church's community center. All of this while working as a part-time youth minister and being a wife and a mother to a young son. You see, Laura gained much of her self-esteem from being needed.

On the other hand, I was the consummate no-man. I said *no* to virtually every request that was thrown my way. I had a commercial driver's license, but I never agreed to drive the children in the after-school program. I was a music major in college, but I never sang in the choir. I ran a multistaff youth ministry, but I never considered running a church board. You see, anytime anyone from the church called I had the word *no* formed in my brain before the question could even be asked. I was very selfish with my time.

It was when Laura and I decided to create a family mission statement that we had to face the music. We needed to lose ourselves in the area of church in order to build our marriage. How did we lose ourselves? Laura chose to give up most of the things that made her overcommitted, and I chose to give more of myself to the church in order to model to my wife and children what a follower of Christ looks like.

As we walked through this "losing" process, we found that Laura most enjoyed being involved on the drama team and that I felt singing was the best I could offer. Together we felt a burden for the youth in our church, so we decided to serve on the youth committee. Are we saying the other activities we were involved in were bad? No. We simply had to give them up in order to do what was best for our marriage, what was best in order to make us one.

Questions for Reflection and Discussion

1. On a scale from 1 to 10, rate how well you lose yourself in your marriage. List some examples.
2. On a scale from 1 to 10, rate how well your spouse loses himself or herself in the marriage. List some examples.
3. Describe how you view marriage. Is it three separate circles: you, your spouse, and the marriage? Or do you view it as two circles intersecting? Give examples of this being fleshed out.
4. Name one area of self that you have been holding onto that could grow your marriage if you let go.

10

Love Your Spouse

Stoking the Flame

The second action needed to bring the facets together is to love your spouse. We read the passage of Scripture that says "become one flesh," and we think this refers to the sex act. But this Greek word goes so much further than just sex. As we lose ourselves, we begin to realize we have more opportunity to love our spouse.

To love your spouse, you have to ask yourself this question: *What do I do every day to show my spouse that he or she is my priority?* Every day. Some type A personalities are already answering this question: "I fill her gas tank and complete her 'honey do' list," or "I cook his meals; I take care of his kids; I clean his house; I iron his underwear." But love is not a checklist. What is it that I'm doing every day to show my spouse that he or she is my priority? How am I losing myself every day to express my love?

> *What do I do every day to show my spouse that he or she is my priority?*

Love in the Grocery Store

A day off! The weekend—what most of us look forward to all week! Time for yourself to do whatever you enjoy. Jay's travel schedule does not allow for many weekends at home. If he takes a day off it is usually Monday. Monday is my grocery shopping day. In order for us to do something together and for the sake of our marriage, he takes his day off and goes grocery shopping with me. Now I tell you, sometimes I secretly wish he wouldn't, but it's the thought that counts. But the point is that Jay will intentionally make time to grocery shop with me. He is thinking not about himself and what he wants to do but about our marriage. Instead of taking that time off for himself, he invests it in our relationship. That's loving your spouse.

I (Jay) have to tell you my true motivation. I travel most of the week for work. After a good night's sleep in my own bed, I'm refreshed. Laura's love language is quality time. (If you haven't picked up Dr. Gary Chapman's book *The Five Love Languages*, get it! It will open your eyes.)* If I want my deep desire for sexual fulfillment met, I need to commit some time to her. There is some selfish ambition on my part. I really don't like grocery shopping, but I know if I spend time to connect with her, she'll desire to connect with me.

When we act this way we begin to meet needs. While loving your spouse is not all about sex, sex is part of the equation. I'm not necessarily talking about sexual intercourse;

---

*Gary Chapman, *The Five Love Languages* (Chicago: Northfield Publications, 1992).

I am talking about intimacy—being and feeling close.

Some of you might be at an age where sex is not part of the equation. Medication, illness, or accident can affect that too. Even if sexual intercourse is rare or not possible, you still

> *Even if sexual intercourse is rare or not possible, you still have to work at closeness, intimacy.*

have to work at closeness, intimacy, maybe even harder because it is a huge part of marriage and of love.

The One Reason Not to Have Sex

We read in 1 Corinthians a message from Paul on marriage:

> Now for the matters you wrote about: it is good for a man not to marry. But since there is so much immorality, each man should have his own wife, and each woman her own husband. The husband should fulfill his marital duty to his wife, and likewise the wife to her husband. The wife's body does not belong to her alone but also to her husband. In the same way, the husband's body does not belong to him alone but also to his wife. Do not deprive each other except by mutual consent and for a time, so that you may devote yourselves to prayer.
>
> 1 Corinthians 7:1–5

There is only one reason why physically capable couples should not be expressing their love for each other through sex, and that is so you can *pray*. Scripture lays out that my body is hers and her body is mine. But here's what I (Jay) find interesting. The husband should fulfill his marital duty to his wife and the wife to her husband. Now a lot of us think the wife's duty to the husband is to have sex. But guys, it also says that we are to fulfill our marital duty to our wives. Gentlemen, understand this: your wife, for the most part, is not ready to jump into bed with you any old time. From our work with couples we know that some women have a higher sex drive than their husband, but for most women that's not the case. In fact, studies show that most women need seven nonsexual, significant touches a day—and no, patting her on the shoulder does not count. Guys, sometimes this is the way we "deprive" our wives.

All of life is a cycle: day, night, summer, fall, winter, spring. What's amazing is that God has designed a holy sex cycle, but he put it together in a very interesting way. For a woman, this holy sex cycle concludes in the physical act of sex. Guys, when that sex act occurs, that's the culmination for your wife. You've been kind, loving, tender, and as a result, those seven nonsexual, significant touches have put her in a place where she's ready to be one with you. Ladies, when you have sex with your man, that is when he wants to be closer to you. He just can't believe that someone as beautiful and as loving as you would want to be with him. That's the start of the holy sex cycle for him.

Sometimes it seems like God's little joke on us, doesn't it? But it's not a joke. Do you know what it means? It means we need each other. What could be more beautiful?

Taking It Further

Now ladies, studies show, again speaking in general terms, that a man needs sex. We know there are men to whom this does not apply, but most men need sexual release every seventy-two hours. That's every three days! Jay made it very clear that he is above average.

> *Most men need sexual release every seventy-two hours.*

I (Laura) know what you are thinking because I have been there myself: *Every three days? I have kids; I have a house; I have a job. You have got to be kidding!* But ladies, shouldn't sex be a pleasurable experience? Does your husband enjoy sex?

If you answer *yes* to both questions, then why not do what it takes to make sure your husband knows he is your priority? If a man, on average, needs sexual release every seventy-two hours, if we're trying to lose our self and love our spouse, if sex should be enjoyable, and if he loves the experience, then why would I not make it a primary concern? I know what happens because I've been there. Everything else comes before him: the kids, the house, the job, the groceries, and the laundry. Actually, those should come after him. Being one, making your spouse your priority, affects every decision you make and every thought you have, whether it has to do with sex or not. Losing yourself and loving your spouse affects every area of your marriage.

Now men, I (Jay) have a couple of questions for you: First, is sex enjoyable? Second (and I don't mean to offend anyone with this next question, but I think we need to be honest), is sex more enjoyable when your wife is into it? I'll tell you my answer: I think sex is much more fulfilling and more pleasurable when she isn't just meeting my needs. So then why wouldn't we men do the little things necessary each day—the kindness, the tenderness, the seven significant touches—to ensure that our wife is in the mood?

What am I doing to make my spouse a priority? It goes far beyond romance and sexuality.

| *So what's at the heart of love for your spouse?* | Discovering the Heart of Your Spouse—Words Guy, Time Gal |

Other than the wonderful romantic and tender moments we share, one of the best ways for me (Jay) to show Laura she is my priority is to spend time with her. It really doesn't have to be anything special. If I drag my big behind off the couch and say, "Let's go for a walk," it screams to Laura, "I love you!" So the heart of my spouse is about spending time together. Work time, play time, any time—just being together.

I on the other hand am a words guy. It means the most to me when Laura says things like: "I love you." "I'm proud of you." "You're a great dad." When she takes the time and energy to verbalize those thoughts, it screams to me that she loves me.

So what's at the heart of love for your spouse? It may take some time for you to discover it, but when you do you will begin to better understand how you can easily and powerfully make your spouse a priority each and every day.

Questions for Reflection and Discussion

1. On a scale from 1 to 10, rate how well you love your spouse. List some examples.
2. On a scale from 1 to 10, rate how well your spouse loves you. List some examples.
3. Give examples of how you show your spouse that he or she is your priority.
4. What is at the heart of love for your spouse? Give examples.

11

Lift the Marriage

Burning Bright

The Dutch have a word, *naaien*, which actually means "to sew together so that it can never be separated." Originally it was a term sailors used to describe the way they sewed sails together. They had to create a strong bond so that the sails could withstand the strong winds and rolling seas of the North Atlantic.

This is also a great way to view marriage. We are sewn together in such a way that we can withstand the strong winds and rolling seas of life. To *lift* the marriage means to make marriage the first priority outside of your relationship with God. When you lift your marriage after losing yourself and loving your spouse, you begin to see a union that operates as one. We are "sewn" together in all five facets of intimacy. It's no longer Jay and Laura but the marriage of Jay and Laura.

> *To **lift** the marriage means to make marriage the first priority outside of your relationship with God.*

The impact of becoming one in our marriages is not some act of masochism that completely wipes out our personalities and disregards who God created us to be. No, it's discovering, maybe for the first time, who God really intended us to be because we are sharing our lives with the partner God designed for us.

Decisions, Decisions!

Lifting the marriage begins with asking the right questions. One of those questions could be, "How are we going to discipline the kids?" I (Laura) grew up in a home where my mom always said, "Just wait until your father gets home." What did she mean? She meant we were in big trouble when Daddy walked through the door because he was going to put the hammer down. Now I use that same phrase in my home, "Just wait until your daddy gets home," but I mean something different. My kids know when they have done something wrong that they will be disciplined after Mom and Dad decide together what the consequence will be. With Jay's schedule, however, that is not always practical and I have to make that decision on the spot. So we have already agreed upon appropriate discipline for misbehavior we can anticipate. For instance, when Grace was younger and had a big dramatic moment and was screaming at the top of her lungs and falling on the floor and kicking her feet, we agreed that she would be sent to her room until she could get control of herself. That's one of the questions we've already answered together for the sake of our marriage.

It would do us all good never to say these phrases again: "Well, here's what *I* think. Here's what *I* would do." We need to use the words *we*, *us*, and *ours* instead of *me*, *my*, and *mine*. Understand that it is a *we* question: What are *we* going to do about disciplining the kids? How are *we* going to make this decision?

A lot of times kids play one parent against the other. For example, our son wants to spend the night at someone's house. In his mind he thinks, *Dad told me that I have to mow the lawn and clean the garage tomorrow. I'd really like to go to Dan's house tonight, so I'll ask Mom.* But that won't work in our family because we have talked about what's going on in our household, and we know that on Saturday we'll have our teenager working his tail off. So my response is, "Yes, son, you can go to Daniel's and stay up late. But at eight o'clock in the morning, you're getting on the lawn mower, Dude." We've already made that decision, so our children cannot play one parent against the other.

You know what the decisions are that you have to make every day whether they are important, urgent, big, or small. Take the time as a couple to be unified in regard to these decisions rather than leaving them for one spouse to handle alone. Decide ahead what is going to be carried out in your marriage.

After hosting a conference in Fort Wayne where we presented this material, we were trying to decide where to eat. Jay asked me, "Where do you want to go?" I replied, "I don't care; you decide." He looked at me incredulously and asked, "Have you heard a word we've said?" I replied, "Nope, obviously not."

Maybe the decision you need to make is more important, like buying a car. The wife may not really care what kind of car they have as long as it's the right color. But if she says, "Honey, buy a red car, nothing else really matters; you decide," she is missing an opportunity to lift the marriage. Learning about horsepower and all-wheel drive, and other automotive issues she may not care about builds intimacy with her husband who does care.

In the same way, he needs to know the difference between ecru and eggshell paint when it comes to interior design because it's important to her. When we care about what our spouse cares about we build intimacy and in turn lift the marriage to the place of importance it truly holds.

Not You or Me, but We!

Lifting your marriage is not erasing who you are. God made you the way you are. The important thing is to mesh who you are with who your spouse is and become a single union. Ask the questions: What are we going to do? How are we going to make this decision?

After a conference Dara came up to me and shared her story: "Laura, my husband and I have always agreed that we will not make any purchase over fifty dollars without consulting the other. I was shopping for running shoes, and I found a pair that fit perfectly. But they cost more than I had expected to spend. So I told the saleswoman, 'I'm going to have to come back tomorrow because I need to talk to my husband.' The saleswoman laughed at me, and said, 'Ma'am, you are ridiculous. Do you have to ask your husband about everything?'"

Dara still went home and talked with her husband. They

> *Lifting your marriage is not erasing who you are. The important thing is to mesh who you are with who your spouse is and become a single union.*

148

agreed that it was fine to spend that kind of money, and she went back the next day to buy the shoes. She considered going somewhere else because the saleswoman had made fun of her, but she went back to the same store. When she walked in, the same saleslady greeted her at the door and exclaimed, "Oh my goodness, you came back. You won't believe what happened. Your shoes are 50 percent off. After you left the store last night my manager told me, 'All the shoes over here have to go on sale 50 percent off,' and I immediately thought of you." Dara said to me, "Laura, God blesses us when we are one."

When we make decisions together, God recognizes our faithfulness to his plan and pours out the blessings. We have to lose ourselves, love our spouse, and lift the marriage.

I know what some of you are thinking. *That is just not practical. I earn a living and pay the bills; she takes care of the kids and the house. We've got it down, boom, boom, boom.* No, it's not practical unless your goal is to fulfill God's purpose for your marriage. He wants us no longer to be separate but to be one.

Being one—the purpose of marriage. Is it practical? Is it possible? We say *yes*. Our small-town newspaper, *The Morning Sun*, in Alma, Michigan, ran a story about a couple who have proven that this union is possible.

When you walk up to Russell and Delia Hanson's front porch near Elwell, Michigan, a sign says, "A nice grandma lives here with an old buzzard." It's not true. The old buzzard, 93, is every bit as nice. Celebrating nearly 72 years of marriage, there is little the couple hasn't done, seen, been through and rejoiced in together. Clearly the romance hasn't faded after all these years. Do they have a secret to their successful marriage?

For one thing, no one ever thought of divorce. Of Russell's seven brothers and sisters and Delia's fifteen siblings, everyone stayed married because that's what you do. But Delia also said they did everything together. When he was out in the field, she was too. And he'd help with the housework, she said. "We always worked together. He sweeps and washes the windows. I think that's what keeps us together, we always work together."

Delia said they weren't like some other couples they know, when they get mad, don't speak to each other for days, although Russell joked, they could do that too. Delia said they don't stay mad at each other. "There are lots of ups and downs, there's always trouble." Do you hear that? Seventy-two years, there's always trouble. "I don't care who you are," Russell said, "all couples can stay married if they try."*

Lift your marriage to the priority position it deserves and watch the sparks fly!

Questions for Reflection and Discussion

1. On a scale from 1 to 10, rate how well you live as if your marriage is more important than you are. List some examples.
2. On a scale from 1 to 10, rate how well your spouse lives as if your marriage is more important than he or she is. List some examples.
3. Is your daily mind-set "I" or "we" as you answer life's questions?
4. What steps can you take to begin thinking more "we"?

*Linda Gittleman, "Rich wth Love," *Morning Sun*, February 2006.

12

Say "I Do"

A Lifetime of Sparks

We all enter our wedding day with many misconceptions of what marriage is really going to be. I (Laura) was petrified, anxious, nervous beyond belief on my wedding day. I thought, *What if I forget what I am supposed to do? What if I do something wrong?* So I made myself a list of three little steps: just walk down the aisle, stand at the altar, and look at him. Walk down the aisle, stand at the altar, and look at him. Aisle, altar, him. Aisle, altar, him. I'll alter him, I'll alter him! There we go, I had it figured out. I knew what marriage was all about: I'll alter him!

Although many new wives think, *Well, I found one I think I can work with,* most men get married hoping their wife will never change: *Oh she loves me, she's young and beautiful, and she actually likes to make out with me.*

When we first got married, life and love were wonderful. We wanted to sustain that, but it's difficult. One way is to say "I do" every day in three very important aspects of life.

Say "I Do" to the *Concept* of Marriage

The first "I do" we want you to say is to the concept of marriage. Earlier in the book I (Jay) told the story of how Laura and I met on a blind date. I wrote about the Atlanta Braves baseball game and how my heart leaped out of my chest when Laura grabbed my hand.

Well to be honest, at the time I really didn't know it was my heart leaping out of my chest. I'm serious; I did not know what that feeling was. In fact, at first I thought it was the hot dogs coming back up for a second round. I found out later because Laura told me, "That's love, buddy." But I couldn't deny I had those feelings where my insides just wanted to explode with joy.

We all remember having those feelings with our spouses. You get married and then five, ten, fifteen days later the excitement fades. You realize you have to work at this thing called marriage.

Did anyone talk to you before you got married? Did they tell you the truth? I wish somebody had slapped me upside the head and told me that I had to work at this thing. It would have solved a lot of issues in our marriage. Unfortunately, many of us just don't like work, so when things become difficult, we think it's time for a change.

Technology is making many tasks in our culture so much easier. With the click of a mouse we can now accomplish tasks that only a few decades ago would have taken hours. When we have problems with the technology all we have to do is ask "Tech Support" for help. It's simply not that easy with marriage. We can't write Tech Support for help.

Tech Support:

Recently, I upgraded from Girlfriend 7.0 to Wife 1.0. I soon had many new issues because Wife 1.0 installed herself into all programs and now monitors all system activity. I can't seem to keep Wife 1.0 in the background while running my favorite applications: Golf 18.0, Football 4.0, Hunting and Fishing 7.5, and Racing 3.6. I'm contemplating going back to Girlfriend 7.0, but the uninstall function doesn't seem to work on Wife 1.0.

Help!
Troubled

I imagine Tech Support writing back, as follows:

Troubled,

This is a very common occurrence. Many men upgrade to Wife 1.0 imagining a utilities and entertainment system. Wife 1.0 is an operating system and is designed by its creator to run everything. It is impossible to delete, uninstall, or purge the program files from the system. I recommend keeping Wife 1.0 and working to improve the situation.

The best course of action is to enter the command C:\ apologize because ultimately you will have to give the apologize command before the system will return to normal. Wife 1.0 is a great program, but it requires much maintenance. Wife 1.0 comes with several wonderful support programs such as Clean and Sweep 3.0, Cook It 1.5, and Do Bills 1.2.

Be very careful, however, how you use these programs. Improper use will launch the program Nag Nag 9.5. Once this happens, the only way to restore the performance of Wife 1.0 is to purchase additional software. I recommend Flowers 1.2 and Diamonds 5.0.

Good luck,
Tech Support

Aren't we glad that God did not create marriage as a computer to be fixed but as two human beings to explore life together?

Before God created marriage he designed the land and the sea, the plants and the trees, the sun and the stars. Then came all the fish of the sea, the birds of the sky, and all the animals. Then he created man. After making Adam, God declared, "That is very good." But then I think he said, "I can do one better." So he created woman!

Adam and Eve were the first married couple, and they never doubted, did they? Adam never looked at Eve and thought, *Hmm, is she all I need? I'm not real sure. Hmm, what if she could be better this way or that way?* And Eve never thought about Adam, *Hmm, I might need to train him a little more.*

Neither one of them doubted. They knew they were enough for each other. They trusted in God, the Creator who made them both, and acknowledged, "I know that my mate is all I'll ever need." Saying "I do" to the concept of marriage means full acceptance that your spouse is all you need.

Saying "I do" to the concept of marriage is also about creating passion, closeness, and desire. There's a great passage of Scripture that says, "Husbands, in the same way be considerate as you live with your wives, and treat them with respect as the weaker partner and as heirs with you of the gracious gift of life" (1 Peter 3:7).

There are some very important ideas in that verse. Reread what it says: "Be considerate as you live with your wives, and treat them with respect." I believe that I need to love my wife, but I also need to respect her. It's not one or the other. She

> *They knew they were enough for each other.*

also needs to love and respect me. It's not one or the other. We're human beings. We live off of both love and respect.

It's the next part of this verse that a lot of people have problems with: "Be considerate as you live with your wives, and

> *Saying "I do" to the concept of marriage means full acceptance that your spouse is all you need.*

treat them with respect *as the weaker partner*" (emphasis added). That's a touchy passage because some men have taken it to mean, "She's the weaker vessel; I'm the stronger vessel, so therefore what I say goes. It's my way or the highway." I just don't read that here.

Fine China

Some ladies don't like being called the weaker vessel. It's not saying that you're weak; it's just saying you're the weaker of the two. "Well, I'm a strong, independent woman." Let me tell you what, I'm married to one of the strongest, most independent women on the planet, but she understands this passage of Scripture.

What this is saying is actually an honor to you ladies. Why? The Greek phrase for *weaker vessel* is actually translated "fine china." Think about that. Ladies, how many of you have a problem being compared to fine china?

Gentlemen, imagine we are walking through an antique store where there are many fine pieces of art and pottery. I take one piece out of the china hutch and say to you, "Sir, this piece of china is very delicate and incredibly expensive. Here, you can hold it." How would you react to that? Some would say, "No thanks!" But if you had the courage to take it, how would you hold and care for that piece? You would hold it gently, tenderly; you would not abuse in any way that piece of fine china, and you would respect its value.

Guys, this is how we say "I do" to the concept of marriage. Realize that God has given you a piece of fine china. She is to be treated with respect, tenderness, gentleness, and care. And as you do that, the passion, closeness, and desire will increase when you see her for the wonderful person she is.

Men Are "Fine" Too

Ladies, I (Laura) think we all would agree that there are times in our husbands' lives that they also are like fine china. They always need to be treated with love and respect, but there are times when they are defeated by their lives, their jobs, their circumstances. That's when they need to be treated with precious care.

I can remember when we were leaving the ministry Jay had known from the time he was born. Through the first ten years of our marriage we had worked side-by-side in this ministry. Then a time came when we felt God was calling us to move into what we're doing now.

But to leave the ministry in which his family was entrenched, step out on faith, and do something totally different was scary. For about a year Jay went through a lot of turmoil and transition even though he knew beyond a shadow of a doubt what the Lord was calling us toward.

At one point during this transition our son, Torrey, and I were taking Jay to the airport. Our habit at the time (this was before 9/11) was to walk with him to the actual ramp to the plane, kiss him good-bye, and watch him board. This particular occasion, as we drove the hour to the airport, we discussed this transition period of our life. We were reflecting back on everything that had been going on that year. As I kissed Jay good-bye, I told him, "Honey, I just want you to know how proud I am of you." Then Torrey and I walked away.

Later that evening Jay called to let us know he had arrived in Miami safely. He said, "Laura, you have no idea what you did to me." Nope, no clue. "I kissed you; what else did I do?" He answered, "Laura, in the ten years we've been married, never once have you told me that you were proud of me." Shot to the heart. His words of deep appreciation convicted me to the core.

There are going to be times in a man's life when he needs to be treated like fine china, with love and respect. I need to be considerate and to love and respect and say the words that he needs to hear. That's how you say "I do" to the concept of marriage.

Say "I Do" to the *Circumstances* of Marriage

If you have a teenager in your home, or if you remember when you were a teenager, you recall what dating is like. We have a teenager in our home who has decided that girls are too expensive and too confusing. Can I (Jay) get an *Amen*? What happens in American culture is that we grow up and learn the dating game. Dating is disposable. Here's my girlfriend this week. Oops, I did something wrong. Here's another girl next week. Oops, I did something wrong. Here's a new girl today. She lasts a day, oops, tomorrow someone new. Dating teaches us that people are disposable, that relationships are disposable. Taken to its logical (or illogical) conclusion, marriage is disposable.

When we say "I do" to the circumstances of marriage, we are saying that there is no circumstance in our marriage that

> *There is no circumstance in your marriage that should dictate the commitment level you have to your marriage.*

will dictate the commitment level of the relationship. I'm going to say that again. There is no circumstance in your marriage that should dictate the commitment level you have to your marriage. When you said "I do," you said "I do" to the circumstances of that marriage.

While working for Youth for Christ, we hosted a marriage workshop at the Grove Park Inn in Asheville, North Carolina. There we met a lovely couple, Lucy and Paul Keller. When we met them, they had been married for twenty years. A year into their marriage, Lucy was involved in a very serious car accident and became a paraplegic. When Paul stood at the altar and said "I do" to the circumstances of marriage, Lucy was standing on both legs. Twenty years later, she was in a wheelchair, but he was continuing to say "I do."

Early in our marriage, Laura had a spending problem that put us in significant debt. I could have condemned her: "Lady, that is your problem. I am so upset with you. You've got to get your act together." But I realized that it's not her issue, it's *our* issue.

And my issues are *our* issues. A survey produced by the Barna Group revealed that in the church, five out of ten men have a serious pornography problem. This means half of men in *church*. I honestly believe that in our modern society every man battles against pornography. You can't turn on the TV without seeing sexual images; you can't open a magazine without seeing things that a man should not see.

As we've worked through this issue in our marriage, Laura could have stood back and said, "You're a gross pig.

I can't believe you." She would have been right. But my pornography problem was not *my* pornography problem, it was *our* pornography problem. We both had to take steps to battle against it.

The first thing Laura did was ask, "What can we do, Jay?" I replied, "Honey, the first thing we need to do is turn off that show you like so much. You know, 'Baywatch.' All the girls are in bikinis, and I shouldn't see that."

When you get married, your spouse's problems are your problems and vice versa. The joy of marriage is in battling those problems, conquering them through strength and trust in the person of Jesus Christ. That, my friends, is saying "I do" to the circumstances.

Examples Paved the Way

Fortunately, in our lives we had two great examples. Jay's parents are wonderful models of growing through the circumstances. A number of years ago Jay's mom broke her leg between the knee and the ankle in ten places. Her bone was shattered. The doctors told her that as little as fifteen years prior to that, they would have had to amputate her leg at the knee because the break was so severe.

Instead they put her in a device called the External Fixator. It consisted of two metal plates with pins sticking through her leg. Her leg looked like a pin cushion with pins sticking out that held the bones in place. Twice a day, every day, my father got down on his hands and knees and cleaned those pins. I watched him work meticulously for hours on end. The doctors told my dad it would take six weeks, so he committed to it.

Those six weeks turned into nine months. Twice a day, every day, my dad cleaned the pins. Finally the doctors declared my mother whole. And if she were to walk through the door of your house, she would not be walking with a limp or a cane. She is a walking miracle. Why? Mom and Dad went through it together.

Another example came from Laura's family. Before our blind date, my friend Chaz told me a little bit about Laura. Her dad had died only a year earlier. When I asked what he died from, he replied, "Everything! He had polio as a child, he was diabetic, and in the last three years he had four heart attacks and three strokes."

Yet in spite of all this, Laura's mom never said, "Oh no, not now. Heart attack number two, I could live with that, but heart attack number three? No, I'm done." She stood beside him, went to work, paid the bills, did whatever it took to make it happen. When you say "I do" to the circumstances of marriage it changes you, and it changes you for the better.

Our good friend Thor Ramsey says this: "One of the best things every couple in America could do to help their marriage would be for the two people to look each other in the face and say these words, 'Divorce is not an option.'" For every couple there are three options when trouble comes: divorce, healing and reconciliation, or living miserably. When you say, "Divorce is not an option," you limit yourself to healing and reconciliation or living miserably the rest of your life. That's not a difficult choice. Again, it is working through that restoration that makes life so exciting and builds intimacy.

Lesson on an Airplane

When I am on an airplane heading home from an event, I just want to curl up in my own little cocoon. Laura calls me an on/off switch; most of the time I'm pretty high energy, but there are times when I'm off. The airplane ride home is a quiet time to recharge my batteries.

One time I was sitting next to a lady who chattered incessantly. By giving her short, one-word answers, I tried to communicate, "I don't want to talk." She didn't get the hint.

Finally I broke down and engaged her in conversation. After finding out what I do for a living, she commented that she was divorced. She continued,

> *For every couple, there are three options when trouble comes: divorce, healing and reconciliation, or living miserably.*

Well, you know, I was young, and I really regret that I did it. I have a couple of kids, fourteen and twelve, and I divorced my husband when they were very young.

When my friends tell me they are considering divorce and there are kids in the house, I smile at them and say, "Okay, I just want to give you a good illustration of what the divorce you're contemplating is going to do to your children: take a baseball bat, line your children up, and hit each of them ten times as hard as you can, the last time in the head, because I know firsthand that's what divorce does to children."

Don't tell me children are resilient. Yeah, they're resilient to the fact that daddy lost his job and we might not have enough money right now. That's okay, Mommy and Daddy, we'll do what needs to be done. Yeah, children are resilient to Dad's job getting changed and we're going to have to move. You're going to have to leave your friends. Don't want to, but okay. But children are not, nor ever will be, resilient to Mom and Dad parting ways.

I didn't realize I would be getting such a graphic picture from a firsthand witness.

Say "I do" to the concept of marriage and rekindle the passion that God gave you. Say "I do" to the circumstances of marriage and allow the Lord to help you become who you were intended to be by walking through daily life together.

Say "I Do" to the *Covenant* of Marriage

A covenant is different from a contract. In America we believe heavily in contracts, but unfortunately we sometimes think of marriage as a contract. A contract is an agreement between two people that has a beginning and an end. A covenant is something that has no end; it is for eternity, and it is said before God and with the blessing of God. When you stood at the altar and said "I do," you made a covenant, much like God made with Abraham when he told him he would make him "the father of many nations" (Gen. 17:4). You are reading this book as a result of that eternal covenant that God made with Abraham.

We partner with a lot of worthwhile organizations; one of them is called the Covenant Marriage Movement. We encourage you to go to www.covenantmarriage.com and check them out. A statement on their website reads,

Too many people today view marriage as a legal contract. Contracts are based on rights and responsibilities and are motivated by self-centeredness rather than unconditional love. A legal contract is necessary to begin, and likewise to end a marriage, but a covenant is more than a contract. It is more than a legal document declaring a state of interdependence.

The value of a "covenant marriage relationship" as opposed to a "contractual marriage agreement" lies in a person's understanding and acceptance of God's intent for marriage and the importance of His presence in that marriage.

One of the women who responded to our survey truly understands God's intent for her marriage even in the midst of a trying situation. Following is her story:

At the core of being one is having the same belief about God, Jesus, the Holy Spirit, and their priority in our lives. The outgrowth is involvement in doing ministry together. Furthermore, we both try to live out the same beliefs that we profess; we also share experiences together (worship, ministry, biblical training of our children).

Three or four years ago my husband revealed a sin to me that he had kept hidden for many years. After he obeyed God and told me and asked me to forgive him (how thankful I am that he was repentant), our marriage blossomed in all areas—God did it all.

It will sound strange, but here goes. The first thing God brought to mind regarding really being one with my spouse was the first time we had sex after my husband repented and I had also forgiven him. It was as if God had said "Be joined together, for this is my gift to you." I am sure this sounds weird to be talking sex here, but I actually believe it was a reward God gave us for being obedient and also an act of worship as we had pledged to stay together and honor God in our marriage.

We have had other times as well when we had to make difficult decisions, so we have prayed separately and together and fasted to find out what God really wanted us to do. There are times when my spouse has revealed to me how he is battling the old nature/flesh, and I understand it completely but with a different life example—he knows I get it and we have that understanding. It is an intensely intimate thing as it's not something everyone else can necessarily relate to or what you would share with just anyone. I know my spouse's most intimate sin challenges.

When All Is Said and Done

One of the radio stations that promotes our marriage conferences ran a contest in which the winner received a free conference registration and hotel stay. Contestants were asked to answer this question: What is your most memorable date? I'd like to share with you one of the responses:

> The most memorable date with my spouse was October 8–9, 2005, when we attended a Celebrate Your Marriage conference. Jerry had a backache as we traveled to Mackinac Island. We laughed, cried, and held each other throughout the weekend. We had a magical, romantic, fairytale weekend and returned home with a renewed love for each other.
>
> On December 9, 2005, sixty days later, Jerry went to be with the Lord. What we did not know then was that Jerry had small cell lung cancer. It was only thirty-one days from diagnosis to death. I love and cherish the memories your conference gave us. Jerry smiles from heaven.

The story does not end there. When we emailed Louise to ask permission to use her story, she gave us this response:

> Jerry and I had our photos taken by the hotel photographer as we went to dinner that evening. We had the photographer also take one picture of us with my 35 millimeter

camera. The hotel photographs turned out absolutely terrible. The week of Jerry's death, my daughter took my film in to be developed. The photo of the two of us was beautiful. The crazy thing was, I knew it would be. I knew God would give me a photo of the two of us on our last date.

That is saying "I do" to a covenant that lasts for eternity. Whether it is for better or worse, for richer or poorer, in sickness or in health, it is 'til death do us part. That is how you say "I do" to a covenant of marriage.

Say "I do" to the concept of marriage, that wonderful, ooey-gooey, passionate feeling you have for your spouse. Say "I do" to the circumstances. No matter where you are on life's journey—the ups and downs, ins and outs—say "I do" to walking through them together as *one*. And say "I do" to the covenant of marriage, 'til death do you part. Here's the stark reality of life. Chances are that one of you, someday, will stand over the casket of the other.

As Laura and I have talked about this, I've told her that if I go first I want her to throw a party! I want it to be fun. Why? Because I'll be looking down from heaven knowing I beat you all.

I don't want people walking by my casket saying silly things like, "He looks so good." That makes no sense to me. I want people to know the single greatest accomplishment I had in my life, so I've asked Laura to simply place a sign on my chest. I started my life with Laura with the words "I Do!" I want the world to know, so that sign in my casket is to read: "I DID!"

That is our prayer for every one of you.

Blessings,

Jay and Laura

Questions for Reflection and Discussion

1. What were the circumstances when you first knew you were in love? How did you feel?
2. How do you keep that feeling alive?
3. Share a time when your marriage encountered rough or rotten circumstances.
4. What principles or practices did you employ to get through that time?
5. Describe your view of a covenant marriage.
6. How do you say "I do" each day?

Survey Results
and Commentary

The following results are from a survey given to over two thousand married people at various Celebrate Your Marriage conferences throughout the country.

The Survey

The typical couple who took our survey was in their midforties and had been married for almost twenty years. Our range in age was quite broad, from twenty-year-olds to octogenarians. Number of years married was similarly broad in range, from newlyweds to those married over sixty years. Finally, our survey looked very much like our country, with many second and third marriages as well as blended families.

On average each day I think about sex _____ *times.*

Our survey indicates that men think about sex nearly two and a half times more often than women. The women in our survey held consistent throughout the age ranges with around 90 percent indicating they think about sex one to two times a day. Men, however vary greatly, with 86 percent of men in their twenties and early thirties thinking about sex five to ten times a day. This drops to 67 percent for men in their late forties and early fifties.

While these numbers may not surprise most people, it is important to note that many of our struggles in marriage come from unmet expectations. (Note that in our work we find that in about 20 percent of the couples the woman has a higher sex drive and thinks about sex more than her husband.)

Early in our marriage, Laura and I faced this situation as I tried to communicate to my Dixie Darling the longing I had to be sexual with her. Laura thinks in pictures, so I challenged myself to come up with a word picture that would appropriately describe my desires. Here was my "brilliant" idea: "Laura, to me, sex is like the air that I breathe." To which she promptly responded, "Then we'd better find you an oxygen tank."

Over the years we had to learn to understand and accept our different views on the frequency of sex in our marriage that resulted from the amount of time each day we thought about the subject.

When I think about being sexual with my spouse, it brings me joy.

In response to this statement, 60 percent of women and 84 percent of men answered at some level of agreement. For the most part, men enjoy sex. Our findings indicate that most men who answered this question to the contrary were experiencing sexual rejection from their wife.

Bob and Barbara had been married for twelve years, had two kids, and on the outside appeared to be happily married. Behind the bedroom doors, however, a different story played out. Barbara had been brought up in a very strict home and was taught by her parents and her church that the primary purpose of sex was procreation. Any thoughts she had about the joy of sex and its role in building a strong marriage were quickly quelled by her nagging childhood and adolescent memories.

Bob confessed that in their marriage he was lucky to have sex with his wife once every two months—usually after a lot of begging and pleading. As a result of the infrequency, their moments of intimacy were just that—moments. This heaped guilt and anguish on the relationship.

Then Barbara began to read Song of Solomon in her personal Bible study. She realized that not once in her upbringing was this book of the Bible actually taught or explained. This revelation provided a light at the end of the tunnel for Bob and gave him hope for their marriage.

Change wasn't quick, and Barbara's past rears its ugly head from time to time. But the frequency and quality of their sex life has them both saying that thinking about being sexual with each other brings them joy.

There are many roadblocks to our sex life.

With very similar responses, 74 percent of men and 76 percent of women agree or strongly agree that there are many roadblocks to sex. This is backed up in our in-depth survey with the resounding answers that money, time, and children are the primary roadblocks.

Sam and Patti homeschool their four children, and Sam works the night shift in order to help out with the schooling. To say these two facts present roadblocks to their sex life is an understatement.

Sam and Patti have tackled these roadblocks head-on with two very practical ideas. First, Patti and her friend Sue, who also homeschools, frequently set play dates for their kids to get together at one house giving the other mom and dad some alone time. Further, Sam and Patti make it a habit to steal away three or four times a year for a night or two.

While these ideas worked for Sam and Patti, the key for any couple to successfully tackle their roadblocks is to work together to create a plan that fits your lifestyle and situation.

Sexual desire is a decision.

Only 38 percent of men, compared with 64 percent of women, believe that desire is a decision. This shows the difference sexually in men and women. For women it is a thought process and for men it is somewhat instinctual—no thinking involved.

We believe this is one of the significant differences for a majority of men and women. While there will be some women for whom sexual desire is instinctual and some men for whom desire must be a decision, by and large this is a process women generally struggle with.

I know it was for me (Laura). Early in our marriage I couldn't believe how often Jay was "in the mood." At first I thought he was abnormally oversexed. But as I listened to my friends talk, it became clear that this was an issue for many of the women I knew.

What changed for us was when I began to fully understand what sex does to and for my husband. I conducted a little experiment with myself. I decided I was going to go the extra mile in our sexual relationship and make desire a decision. I regularly focused my attention throughout the day on Jay and what a wonderful man he is. After the kids were in bed I bathed, rubbed good-smelling lotion on my freshly shaved legs, and put on something that made me feel sexy. I was amazed how these simple actions changed my mood.

Now don't get me wrong, this isn't an everyday experience. But the longer we are married, the more I can pick up on the subtle cues that occur when Jay needs me to be there for him sexually. It is at that point that I make desire a decision and take the necessary steps to meet his needs.

I communicate about sexuality issues with my spouse.

Interestingly enough, in the under-twenty-five age bracket, 61 percent talk about sex daily or weekly. This diminishes to 36 percent in the fifty-six and older age bracket.

It is not surprising that communication about sexuality diminishes with age, much like the proclivity for sex. However, communicating about sexual issues is critical to a healthy marriage relationship. It is said that if you can't communicate in the bedroom, you won't be able to communicate in any other room of the house.

Men and women must learn to communicate in caring and mature ways not only about frequency issues but also about the ways in which we can please each other. Communicating in a respectful and tactful way can unlock romance and passion, allowing for a deeper, more fulfilling lovemaking experience.

Of our respondents, 22 percent only talk about sex once a year, and 5 percent never talk about sex. No doubt this is a formula for disaster and disillusionment in a marriage. Even if a couple is not having sex because of age, medication, illness, or injury, it doesn't preclude the need to talk about sexuality issues that exist in every marriage.

I feel comfortable sharing my desires with my spouse.

Less than half, 43 percent of women and 44 percent of men, are comfortable sharing their desires on a regular (frequent, often) basis. And 19 percent seldom or never feel comfortable.

John and Connie have been married for over forty years, and to look at them you would say they had a great relationship. John frequently bought flowers or a card for Connie. He held the door for her, helped her with her coat, and generally treated her like a queen. Only one thing was wrong with this picture: the words "I love you" had not come out of John's mouth for years.

One day out of the blue, John confided to Jay, "I wish I could tell Connie what she really means to me. I wish I could put into words the way I feel." When John was growing up, he was taught that *real men* don't share their feelings, especially feelings that express love or romantic emotion. John had been wrestling internally for years with the voice of his father and his father before him. As John grew older, he confessed he didn't want his life to end without taking the steps necessary to verbally communicate his deep love for Connie.

Through much thought and prayer, John won the battle within. He went to the local flower shop, bought a dozen roses, and addressed the card to Connie but wrote nothing on the inside. He drove home and delivered the flowers to his bride. When she opened the card she was a bit confused. At that point, he took her by the hand, looked her square in the eyes and began to communicate all the feelings he had for her and his desires for their marriage in its later years. He finished with those three little words that mean so much: "I love you."

I discuss sexuality issues with my friends.

71 percent of women and 39 percent of men discuss sexuality issues with their friends—*hold this thought as you proceed to the next question.*

I see talking with my friends about sexuality issues as a violation of my marriage covenant.

We found that 64 percent of men and 56 percent of women feel it is a violation. For those over fifty-five years of age, 81 percent of men and 73 percent of women see this as a violation.

We asked these questions because we believe our culture has made it fashionable to discuss intimate issues openly. Most of us would find it repulsive to even think about bringing another person into our marriage bed, yet we readily bring others' opinions into the marriage bed. Much of what takes place in the bedroom between a husband and wife needs to stay in the bedroom.

While it is difficult to talk openly and honestly with a member of the opposite sex about sexuality issues, it is in this conversation that a husband and wife find sexual freedom and fulfillment. In most relationships, ours included, one is more sexually adventurous than the other. As we have grown in our marriage, Laura has learned when to tell Jay, "Ain't no way."

On the other hand, we want to make allowance for practical issues that men and women face. For example, I (Jay) have a small number of close male friends who have agreed to ask each other the tough questions about lust, pornography, and masturbation. This discussion is not a violation of the marriage covenant but is done to make the marriage bond stronger. In the same vein, Laura has a couple of friends who are struggling with the challenges of menopause and the strain it places on their marriage bed. Their conversations are about frank and practical ways to meet these challenges.

In conclusion, we challenge you to ask the question, "Is the discussion I am having with my friends helping me love my spouse more, or does it more closely resemble a TV talk show?"

My feelings influence my ability to be sexual.

95 percent of women and 61 percent of men agree.

Laura and I love to tease! We love to poke fun at each other in good-natured ways. Early in our marriage I started calling Laura my "left-handed freak of nature" because she is left-handed and does freaky things. For instance, she frequently opens doors into her head. How can that be? For a left-handed person living in a right-handed world, it is easy! But I know I have a crossed a line from endearing teasing to hurting her feelings when she says, "That was mean."

My male friends can call me short, fat, bald, and ugly, and I will give it right back. But if Laura were to say these things, it would really hurt. In any marriage, when we cross the line and hurt feelings we put up a barrier to intimacy.

My spouse values my feelings regarding our sex life.
85 percent of men and 92 percent of women agree.

I value my spouse's feelings regarding our sex life.
93 percent of men and 96 percent of women agree.

These two survey questions and the overwhelmingly positive responses give us great hope. As couples identify, respect, and honor each other's feelings, it builds a healthy foundation for a growing sexual relationship.

Rank your level of satisfaction with regard to sex in your marriage.
45 percent of women and 47 percent of men rank their satisfaction 8 or higher.

21 percent of women and 15 percent of men rank their satisfaction 4 or less.

By far the most popular answer from all those taking the survey was 10 in all age brackets. However, it is our experience that most respondents had a romantic (sexual) evening the night before taking this survey, so perhaps this is a bit skewed.

Rank your spouse's level of satisfaction in regard to sex in your marriage.
59 percent of women rate their husband's satisfaction at 6 to 10.

62 percent of men rate their wife's satisfaction at 6 to 10.

13 percent of women and 10 percent of men give it the highest level of satisfaction.

Again, the romantic evening before taking the survey might affect these responses.

My expectations are _____ compared to my spouse's expectations.

Of the respondents, 26 percent reported equal expectation levels towards sex. This indicates somewhat healthy communication in this area, which is key to a healthy sex life.

The Wilsons love to work in the yard together. Spending a sunny afternoon mowing, raking, and pruning is not only great recreation for them but a time to connect as a couple. As Joan nears sixty, she has felt the hands of time sap her stamina. She can no longer keep up with Rodney in the physical exertion department.

They shared a story of a wonderful afternoon filled with time together in the yard. Joan could see "the spark" in Rodney's eye, which communicated to her that he was going to want to continue this fun-filled afternoon with a fun-filled evening of romance. It was at that point Joan had to communicate her expectations to Rodney. "Dear, if you are expecting me to have any energy later on tonight, then we need to let the rest of the lawn work wait until another day." With that simple statement, Rodney put away the lawn tools and sent Joan in for a nap!

Communication about sexual expectations may not always be that simple, however it is worth the effort and can be a wonderful way to meet each other's needs.

Further information from this question indicates 55 percent of men showed greater expectations compared to only 15 percent of women. This statistic trends closely with national averages, which show men have a higher sex drive than their wives.

My sexual relationship with my spouse affects my relationship with the Lord.

Only 56 percent see our sex life affecting our relationship with the Lord. But notice the responses to the next question.

My relationship with the Lord affects my sexual relationship with my spouse.

74 percent agreed that our relationship with the Lord affects our sex life. We believe this is strong support of the idea that Christian couples do not see the correlation between their sex life and their spiritual life. How can I expect to have quality quiet time with my Lord when I am not having quality quiet time with my spouse, and vice versa. We Americans compartmentalize so well! We simply don't see how one area of life can impact every other area.

Let's use a simple illustration like caffeine. Caffeine is a wonderful stimulant that helps millions of people wake up in the morning! However if taken in excess, caffeine can negatively impact us mentally, physically, and, yes, spiritually by causing our hearts and minds to race too fast to focus on the Lord.

In the same way, our survey showed that our walk with the Lord impacts our sex life. Similarly our sex life impacts our walk with the Lord. Healthy sexuality involves focusing more on the other person than on yourself. This is a basic tenet of our faith. Therefore a healthy sex life can make us more like Jesus in the same way that an unhealthy sex life can make us less like Jesus.

We do not find it ironic that some of the most prolific writing concerning marriage found in Scripture is preceded by this passage: "And *whatever you do*, whether in word or deed, *do it all* in the name of the Lord Jesus, giving thanks to God the Father through him" (Col. 3:17, emphasis added).

I believe marital sexual issues are a problem in the church.

85 percent of those responding agreed or strongly agreed. We must begin to address this issue in our churches.

I believe marital sexuality issues are being properly addressed in the church.

Of the respondents, 85 percent did not feel the church is properly addressing marital sexuality issues. Our research indicates that marital problems are an issue in the church. We are seeing trends indicating Christian marriages are ending in divorce at rates similar to the national average. This trend should disturb virtually every follower of Christ.

We must confess that for many years we felt as if the church did not care about marriage. After numerous conversations with pastors from virtually every denomination, however, we have come to the conclusion that the church *does* care about marriage; it is just not sure what to do. The good news is that this problem is solvable.

In our conversations with pastors, we have found that most couples who struggle share some common themes:

"We are Christians; we are not supposed to have problems."

"Your proposed solution requires too much work."

And for many second marriages:

"If I had known marriage was this much work, my first marriage probably would not have ended in divorce."

We believe that the church and the millions of couples who follow Christ are now seeking practical, real-world applications to grow their marriage. This is why we are extremely excited about many emerging marriage initiatives similar to our Marriage Champion program. Much like the youth ministry boom of the '60s and '70s and the emergence of men's and women's conferences and movements of the '80s and '90s, we firmly believe the American church is on the cusp of a new and exciting way to educate, enrich, and equip marriages.

Take Our Survey

After conducting and evaluating our survey research on intimacy we had a bit of a revelation. It occurred to us that the problem with most books on intimacy is that, much like our survey, they focus solely on the physical side of the relationship. After much research, prayer, and looking intently at our own relationship, we developed the concept of the five facets of intimacy. The fact is that intimacy is experienced and can be deepened in five significant areas of a marriage relationship.

To assist us in writing this book, we asked people to take an in-depth survey online to share with us their perspective on the different facets of intimacy in their marriage. Below are the questions we ask online. As you read these questions and ponder your answers, we invite you to go to www.celebratenet.com/sparksurvey and take this survey as well. Your answers may be used to help others in future books, workshops, and conferences.

In-Depth Survey

Mental

1. How do you and your spouse connect on a mental level?
2. In what ways do you and your spouse mentally stimulate each other?
3. Do you and your spouse differ mentally?
4. How do you best learn?
5. How does your spouse best learn?
6. Describe a moment when you felt mentally intimate with your spouse (when it was as if you were thinking the same thoughts).
7. When given a specific subject matter, such as sports, politics, parenting, I know what my spouse is thinking _____ percent of the time.
8. On a scale of 1 to 10 (low to high), rate your mental intimacy with your spouse.
9. Over the years of your marriage, how have you seen this area change?

Social

1. How would you describe you and your spouse's social life?
2. Are you compatible socially, or do you find that you prefer to do you own thing?
3. How often do you date each other?
4. What do you do when you date?

5. What are some obstacles that keep you from dating more often?
6. Do you have more friends as a couple or individually?
7. Do you spend more time in social settings alone or with your spouse?
8. Describe a moment when you felt socially intimate with your spouse.
9. On a scale of 1 to 10 (low to high), rate your social intimacy with your spouse.
10. Over the years of your marriage, how have you seen this area change?

Emotional

1. How do you and your spouse connect on an emotional level?
2. Do you share feelings with each other on a regular basis, or do you find that you keep feelings inside? Why?
3. Does your spouse empathize with your feelings (I feel what you feel)?
4. How do you share feelings with your spouse? List some of the words you use when sharing feelings.
5. On a scale of 1 to 10 (low to high), rate your emotional intimacy with your spouse.
6. Over the years of your marriage, how have you seen this area change?

Physical

1. Define physical intimacy.
2. Would you say you are fulfilled physically in your marriage? Why or why not?
3. Are you more touchy-feely or more hands-off?

4. Is your spouse more touchy-feely or more hands-off?
5. When physically intimate, who generally initiates the encounter?
6. Has health, injury, or age had an impact on your physical intimacy? For how long? In what ways?
7. What motivates you to be physically intimate with your spouse?
8. On a scale of 1 to 10 (low to high), rate your physical intimacy with your spouse.
9. Over the years of your marriage, how have you seen this area change?

Spiritual

1. How would you describe your spiritual life? Your spouse's?
2. Define spiritual intimacy.
3. How do you stay spiritually intimate with your spouse?
4. Do you pray together? Worship together? Read Scripture together? Have the same views on tithing? Fast together? Serve together?
5. Describe a moment when you felt spiritually intimate with your spouse.
6. On a scale of 1 to 10 (low to high), rate your spiritual intimacy with your spouse.
7. Over the years of your marriage, how have you seen this area change?

A Note from the Authors

In chapter 1 we shared that we are passionate followers of Jesus. That statement means different things to different people: some think of it as organized religion, others think it means they are "spiritual," and others can only think in terms of how they were raised in faith. To avoid any confusion, we want to briefly share what following Jesus means to us.

Let's start at the beginning: we believe that there is a God who created heaven and earth and that he did so in six days, resting on the seventh. Did those days look like our twenty-four-hour time segments? We don't know, but we do believe there is a God who made everything.

What's interesting is how he made everything. The Bible says "he spoke" and the sun, stars, earth, sea, and creatures of all kinds came into being. That being the case, we are looking at one amazing God, since he only had to speak and the universe was formed.

Now what he did next is very odd. For his final creation he did not speak. Instead he reached his hand down and from the dust of the earth formed this creature, then he "breathed into his nostrils the breath of life" (Gen. 2:7) and in turn gave humans something he gave no other creature—an eternal soul.

God's design for humans? That we would live forever in the presence of God himself. That first man had a choice, however, and when he chose sin over God, that nature began to be handed down genetically throughout the generations all the way to us. The challenge for us, then, is that this genetic nature (written deeper than any microscope can probe) will eternally separate us from God, whose intent was to live with us forever. To the human problem of sin, God chose a supernatural response in the person of Jesus.

Jesus Christ, the God-man born of an earthly mother and heavenly Father, lived a sinless life and claimed to be God incarnate, God in the flesh. He proved this not only by the way he lived and the miracles he performed but by conquering death and rising from the grave.

All of this was done so that sin would not separate God and man anymore. Jesus's perfect life, death, and resurrection were God's way of showing grace. *Grace* is not getting what we deserve. We all deserve separation from God (hell) because of the sin of our first father (Adam) passed on through generations to our own sin. But because of the work of Jesus, we are spared that separation.

What does it mean to follow Jesus? Simply put, life is a journey with one of two destinations: heaven (eternity in the presence of God) or hell (eternity separated from God). The only way to spend eternity with God is by receiving the grace of Christ and choosing to follow him daily. How does this journey begin? With a simple prayer of repentance.

If you have never received the grace Christ offers and desire to do so, we invite you to pray this simple prayer in your heart and begin a journey with Christ today:

> God in heaven, it's _____ [insert your name], and I realize right now that sin in my life stands between me and an eternity with you. God, I wish to turn from that sin and ask the grace found in Jesus to cover that sin. I long to follow Jesus and live forever with you. Amen.

The journey following Christ is not simply praying the prayer above. It involves maturing into the spiritual being that God intends you to be. Is it easy? Not if you try to do it on your own. But it is easy in that God is ready to assist you each and every day through some very practical and yet mysterious ways. First, he provides the Holy Spirit. Jesus promised that when we receive his grace he will send his Spirit to live in our hearts and guide our daily lives. So listen to his voice. Second, he gives us his Word, the Bible. It is a blueprint for life; immerse yourself in it in order to better understand his way. Finally, we have fellowship with other believers. Where can you interact with and learn from other believers? It's called the church. Yes, we believe that corporate worship and praise are critical to the maturity of anyone following Christ. You cannot do it alone.

So do we do a perfect job of following Christ every day? Not at all. We are still human, still prone to the old genetic code of sin. But with Christ's help we strive to mature into the people God intends us to be.

If you have further questions about what it means to follow Jesus, email us at info@celebratenet.com.

Becoming a Marriage Champion

In talking with pastors and ministers across the country, we have found that there is a deep need for couples who desire to champion the cause of marriage in their

- home
- church
- community

In response to this need, we have developed a web-based program designed to inspire, train, and equip couples around the country to champion the cause of marriage.

This program is putting resources and tools into the hands of hundreds of couples who are having an impact on the world for Christ through strengthening marriages and families. For more information, or to become a marriage champion, visit www.celebratechamps.com.

Jay and Laura Laffoon believe marriage was meant to be a full-contact party! Jay and Laura give couples permission to celebrate and show them how to live with respect, ceremony, and festivity.

The Laffoons' unique and motivating seminars have been shared throughout the United States and Canada. Their presentations are full of humor, real-life experiences, and biblical truth. Couples walk away challenged and enriched.

After meeting on a blind date in 1984, that fun-filled evening in Atlanta, Georgia, has turned into years of marital celebration. Ministering together in Youth for Christ for fifteen years, the Laffoons gained tremendous insight into marriage and family issues. Jay and Laura will encourage, inspire, and challenge you to celebrate your marriage.

Jay grew up in Petoskey, Michigan, and attended Taylor University, graduating with degrees in biblical literature and music. He served as an executive director in Youth for Christ for fifteen years. Jay is a certified instructor with Dynamic Communications International. He was twice named an Outstanding Young Man of America.

Laura grew up in Atlanta, Georgia, and graduated from Belhaven College in Jackson, Mississippi, with a degree in social ministries. She too is a certified instructor with Dynamic Communications International and received Youth for Christ USA's Presidential Award for Excellence in Youth Ministry in 1997.

Jay and Laura live in Alma, Michigan, with their seventeen-year-old son, Torrey, and ten-year-old daughter, Grace.

They founded Celebrate Ministries, Inc., in 1995.

Visit thesparkbook.net for these resources:

- video message from the authors

- free downloadable leader's guide

- complimentary participant notes

- and more tools to keep the sparks flying!

BakerBooks
a division of Baker Publishing Group
www.BakerBooks.com